Under t

By Jean Marie Wilbert

Table of Contents

Dedication

I dedicate this to my husband, three children, and my family. Thank you for always listening and believing in me. It has been a roller coaster ride. I would not change a thing.

(Except for names. The names have been changed to protect the innocent. The stories are all true to the best of my knowledge.)

Also to my clientele, employees, and friends who never stopped talking, laughing, and inspiring me in my personal space and behind the chair.

Is the heat ever too hot?

Love and Peace

Acknowledgements

I am of the age – in years and wisdom – where reflection becomes an essential element of nurturing the world around me. Most people say "never go back" but in my world you have to look back to see ahead. Years of hard-fought accumulation of knowledge have forged themselves into experience, and experience has blossomed into wisdom. My gift stems from my ability to make sense of the world, to make peace within myself, and then to share that sensible peacefulness with my people. It is through that framework that I offer the reader these musings.

Life is like a puzzle. Every piece is perfectly placed. We often don't feel that way in the moment but when we reflect with an open heart and wide eyes, it's all there. Our every experience is a puzzle piece, and every moment locks into the next, creating a solid explanation of how we got to this present place.

When I was a younger woman I insistently complained about my life. I griped about my parents. I blamed everyone else for my misgivings. A series of savage lessons led me to the understanding that I own my destiny. I am wholly responsible for, not what happens to me, but how I handle it. Now I see with new eyes, every experience as good and challenging.

My childhood was pretty dysfunctional. Flawed coping mechanisms followed into my young adult years and aided in two divorces, loss of friendships, and even broken family relationships.

The hair salon ended up being a place of comfort. My employees were family to me. The clients embraced me. The experience built me. The lessons molded my understanding of life by building confidence, connections, commitment, and joy. I never regret one day going into work because I knew I was going to laugh, talk and share stories all day long. It became this place of community.

My children spent many hours in the salon, my oldest daughter worked the front desk and youngest daughter did the towels and eventually worked the front desk too. My son, well, he just hung out – occasionally of his own will!

My oldest daughter Melissa and I, pretty much grew up together. I was a young mom and no doubt made so many mistakes, but she is resilient. She teaches me unconditional love. Her mere presence made me responsible, but her unique quality of vibrant joy taught me grace. This woman knows how to love. Her devotion to her own family inspires me to this day. She is a mother and a fine one, at that. She has patience, wisdom, and so much love. I am proud of her immensely.

My son, Blayne, is such a joy. He was a mama's boy until he hit high school. He always wanted to sit by me everywhere we went. He taught me that laughter is the best medicine, that everyone is different, and has their own path. He has been one of my biggest teachers in this life. His sufferings are my sufferings but through his tenacity he is stronger than I ever was at his age.

My youngest daughter Saige, has always been driven. She wanted to be at the salon growing up even if she just sat in a chair next to my station so she could listen to everyone. She learned a lot being at the salon. She grew up fast because of it. Her work ethic to this day is exceptional. She has taught me to stay focused, driven, and passionate. Her love is pure and I am proud of her and her accomplishments.

My husband Terry has been my foundation from the day I met him. He truly has embraced my children and me from day one. His love for my children has been uplifting. We make a great team. I will forever be grateful for his strength and support through all my endeavors. Our love is strong and it just gets better every year.

I have had so many great friends over the years but I have to start with this one. Denise Neal - she encouraged me to write this book for over twenty years ago. I will always hold her friendship dear to me.

If it wasn't for the Oprah's 2020 Vision Tour, I would not have taken this out of the closet and dusted it off. She said dream bigger than you have ever dreamt. So, this is my dream, growing and becoming bigger than I ever thought possible.

Last, but not least - Meg Langlitz. She is a friend, editor, and great supporter through this. There was so much serendipity on how this all came together. I know we are always right where we are supposed to be.

It starts with a seed we either water or let die. I almost let this book die because of fear and doubt, but I kept it for twenty years, knowing one day it would come to life when I was brave enough.

The heat was never too hot under the dryer.........

Prologue: Dream Stealers

I breathed in the sweet scent of my newborn, kissed her fuzzy head, and headed back into the aromas of hairspray and perm that vitalized and supported me. In my heart I was rejoining a job and community I knew well before maternity leave, but I did not reseat myself into my existing spot in anyway other than on paper. The salon moved, my coworkers had turned over, the owner was suddenly absent, her slightly creepy husband was around more often than I thought necessary. I was given my own set of keys to the salon and had the freedom and trust to come and go whenever I needed. I locked up most nights. There is a level of independence I should have appreciated, but something felt off. It was a little like I was abandoned and while not afraid of the solitude, I was not entirely comfortable with it either.

The owner's flashy husband would stick his jet black, slicked back head of hair in and take a gander, smile his enormous blinding white toothed grin, wink at the crew, and just as quickly slink away leaving a cloud of two-dollar cologne in his wake. Confused looks were always exchanged, but we shrugged him off as one more weird character in the biz.

It was the day that the owner burst through the doors, pointed her bubble gum pink manicured fingers at a few of us, motioned to the backroom, and frantically accused us of stealing out of the cash register that I started to rethink my need for this job.

"Maybe you should be around more if you're worried about what goes on here," I blurted.

I had just enough going on in my life, between midnight feedings, school drop off lines, and all the other things it takes to keep a family of five afloat, that I did not have the spoons to put up with this garbage. She slowly looked me up and down, marking me as her prey.

The effect her outburst and accusation had on us was equal parts suspicion, paranoia, and just plain annoyance. *This is no way to live,* I thought as I latched on to departing clients at the end of the day, making sure to never be caught alone, looking twice at coworkers who passed by the register or lingered too long in the backroom. I felt the darting eyes of others hoping to catch the thief and felt the nastiness of a group of cats hunting a rat.

Just enough time passed for the atmosphere to relax a bit when in comes that husband of hers. I noted his swagger, jeans (ironically) too tight to hide anything, button shirt draped open enough to show a patch of hair the size of the rodent we'd been looking for. I eyed him as I walked my client back to the shampoo bowl. It sits nestled behind a wall that obscured me from his view. He must have craned his slimy neck around, and assumed he was in the clear because when I got an inkling to see what he was up to, I caught a sight of him hastily digging in the cash register and shoving wads of cash into his stupid jeans. I gasped as I thought HOLY SHIT, he's the one stealing! Her own husband. I whipped back around the wall and clapped my hand over my mouth.

A mix of rage at him, elation at solving the crime, and pity for the betrayed owner overtook me. But, what should I do? Will I be believed? I polled safe subjects and was not coming up with a consensus.

A few days pass, and there he is again. This time I recruited a coworker to stealthily keep watch with me. The two of us, sleuths in action, managed to witness his crime (while creating perfect bobs on our clients). We agreed that the other girl knew the owner better and should be the one to tell. She was as apprehensive as I was about being blamed, but was fueled by the fury of this man's audacity.

The owner crashed through the door the next day with the ferocity of a woman scorned. Unfortunately for me, she was certain I was the scorner. Like the scoundrel he was, that husband convincingly denied his crime and turned her on me and the other girl. She was filled with rage from so many directions, that there was no talking to her, no defending myself, no clearing my good name.

"Fess up, I know it's you!" her voice billowed out of the breakroom. Every eye in the place was searing into me through the walls.

I tried to use logic and reason and evidence, but the more I said, the more wrath flashed in her eyes. At some point the pressure transformed me from a confused lump of coal into a diamond of bitchiness. I took a deep breath, solidified that I would not have a job after this, and returned her fire.

"You are living in a fantasy world! Your husband is a thief and a creep! Your life is a sham! Your business sucks!" I shouted for the salon to hear. Any sympathy I had felt in the beginning was ashes under my fuming feet. I stormed out, collected my stuff and myself and shouted, "I QUIT" as if my volume could push away all of her nastiness and shameful accusations. I fumbled the key off my ring and threw it at her in one last display of dominance before I broke down in the solitude of my car, heading for home. I allowed myself the space of one commute to feel broken, wronged, shamed. I let despair leach into bitterness then seethe into hatred, but by the time I pulled into my drive, I was smiling. Resilience had won out.

I knew immediately what my next step would be. I wasn't done trembling and sobbing before I had solidified the plan in my mind. I would own my own salon. I would never work for anyone again. I would never be subject to irrational dumpster fires of incompetence and hysteria.

I was intoxicated with the idea of creating my own thing. I entered my house as a boss – in spirit if nothing else. Yet.

In the long bubble bath I receded into that night, details were cemented, dreams were secured. The next morning, I informed my husband of our new journey and he informed me that it was indeed my journey and mine alone. It stopped me for a beat as I sorted through some of the assumptions I had made, then served as an untethering of sorts. Indeed, it was my journey – all mine.

I began the research, the groundwork, the adventure of figuring out the details and pulling them all together. As material steps coalesced and I knew this bird would take flight, I began to tell everyone. I sang my vision to anyone who would listen. My thoughts and actions were wrapped up in this fledgling vision. I felt the exuberance my inner circle shared for me, that altruistic joy real friends feel for their people.

But as human nature goes, this story is not about them. Instead, it calls out the two people who fell short of that lovely zephyr, that robbed me of the wind that was to give lift to my feathered dream. I called them the "Dream Stealers."

"Dad!" I effervesced, "I have big news!" I laid out my vision and plan with all of the gusto of a girl ready to fly and he met it with the monotone dousing of, "I'm not giving you any money."

"No, no, I'm not asking for any. I'm telling you that I'm going to do this." The optimism was waning, but I wasn't giving up on it yet.

"You don't know anything about owning a business," he guffawed.

"I will learn." The smile on my face is the only part of me not sinking.

"You will fail." He purposefully locked eyes with me and seared this message into my being. "And I won't help you," he added after an unbearable silence.

"I'm not asking." The smile is in freefall.

"Why are you telling me?" he asked in honest disillusion.

"Because you're my dad and I thought you would be proud of me." Each word was a brick in the wall I was building between us.

"I think it's a stupid idea. I think you're not smart enough to run a business."

My bird is spiraling.

I found my way out of that interaction, took to my car, and cried my way home as had become the custom. *That hurt*, I allowed myself to feel. But proving one hater wrong (who is, no secret, a grumpy old man, armed with the audacity only a dad can have toward his daughter) was my fuel. I will get this right if only to prove him wrong, I told myself.

Just as I was dusting myself off, I was sucker punched again.

A Phoenix Suns game with friends offered a dose of jubilant comradery. Our double date was full of laughter and catching up, and of course me gushing about my salon. It felt good to say. *My* salon. The wife of the couple met my enthusiasm by leaping up from the table and wrapping me in a hug that was punctuated by our bouncing and squealing together in each other's embrace. This is what it means to be alive. This is a celebration. I was back in the sky.

"I'll make a bathroom and beer run," I said after all of the construction dates and opening details had been shared.

"I'll join you," the girlfriend's husband announced and followed me out of our seats and into the bustling breezeway of the arena. As we were standing in line, he abruptly turned to me and said, "You have no right to start a business. You're a *woman*!"

I whipped my head around to face him, and proclaimed, "WTF?!?"

He kept on, "Who do you think you are? You know nothing. You have small kids. It takes work. You know nothing," he scolded.

I stood there, mouth ajar while he took the opportunity to drive home his message, "You know nothing. You know nothing." He repeated this until I gathered my shit and spat back at him, "Watch me prove you wrong."

My blood was boiling, my heart was racing. Of all people, I thought he would support me, we are friends, he had a successful business (given to him by his daddy). I grabbed our beer and walked back to our seats and never said a word.

All I knew was that I was going to show those two how a woman can get things done.

There is an odd irony in having someone pluck your dream from the air. It crushes you. It grounds you just as you were departing the mundane dirt beneath your feet. It adds violence to your jubilee. But in that, it also sharpens you. It alerts you to the watching eyes and the awaiting scavengers, those that revel in others' failure, or that can't see past their own.

Adore Hair Salon opened September 21, 1994 and it was successful for 11 years. I employed 18 -21 employees at any given time, four nail technicians, a massage therapist and three receptionists, including my daughters Melissa and

Saige. My older sister, Diane, helped over the years as well. I had numerous hairdressers work for me the first few years, but to my great pride, after a few years I had employees that stayed for up to 10 years. We became family. We traveled to hair shows together, went to weddings, celebrated birthdays, graduations, and divorces together. I measure my successes in the typical business metrics of size, growth, and profit, but also in the number of hugs, laughs, and friends I made along the way.

I define all other endeavors by the sense of pride I developed as owner of that salon. It allowed me to control my life. It kept me financially secure through my second divorce. It kept me surrounded by my people. It kept me in charge of my own destiny. I created a place where folks could gather and be and leave, feeling beautiful and connected.

The Little Brown Bag

"Crazy, wild free…. And that just describes my hair."

-Luvlyl Long Locks

"Stella, did you bring your breakfast with you this morning?"

I eye the spunky woman sitting alert in the salon chair, draped in a flashy silk blouse, guarding the neatly folded brown paper bag in her lap.

Silence.

Stella glances around the salon with an unrevealing and distant interest in the other patrons. She eventually offers up a slight smirk, drawing her thin lips into an off-center show of self-amusement. Her eyes flicker up to meet my inquisitive and slightly annoyed gaze, displaying the full force of her feisty demeanor. This is a woman who approaches each moment with the playfulness of a kitten and the venom of a viper.

I'm no meek bunny and meet the moment with equal intensity and a matching sneer. My interest is piqued.

"When are you ever speechless?" I questioned sarcastically. Stella had never missed the chance to own the spotlight or share a piece of scandalous information.

With the heir of a not-quite-benevolent queen, Stella turns her gaze to her reflection in the station mirror. She lifts her chin, admiring her ability to make me squirm.

I grit my teeth, purse my lips, feel the frustration start to rise, and grumble, "What's up with you?" And then as an indignant afterthought I add, "And what's in the bag... Is it top secret or something?"

Stella coyly cocks her head.

"Do you have Sal's dentures in there? Better yet, his ashes? Want me to help you decide what to do with them?" I pivot, addressing Stella's reflection now in the familiar salon arrangement.

"Very funny, dear," Stella pipes through pussy cat pink lips.

I side step, swiveling the chair to look her directly in her flickering eyes. "What is in the bag," I ask flatly. "You look like you're guilty of something."

"Okay," Stella concedes, drawing the moment out just long enough to force my hands to my hips. Stella can be a bit dramatic. I certainly can too.

Stella finally launches into a hushed chronicle of her teenage years, followed by seemingly superfluous details of her twenties, then onto an overly elaborate account of her thirties. I tune her out somewhere after a hair color change and silently long for the awkward silence of the previous few minutes.

Registering a pause, I refocus my attention on the bag. Then, like a snowball rolling into a landslide I start to piece together key words from her narrative and it hits me. It hits me very hard.

Stella picks up her story again, "It's time to go back to my thirties." I look around the salon frantically. No, no, no. This can't be happening here.

Stella's story now requires the use of her hands, so she relinquishes her hold on the neatly folded bag in order to accentuate some detail.

Oh. Dear. God. There they go.

The bag tips and spills out, revealing the secret cascading down Stella's lap, then onto the floor of my station.

"They'd better be clean," I shout.

"Shut up dear, I don't want anyone to know," Stella pride fully begs.

"KNOW?!" I bring my hands to my face in a rush of frustration, embarrassment, and shock. I take in the image of Stella's lap, legs, and my stall floor littered in tufts of five-inch-long pubic hairs.

Silence again.

"Why did I get into this business?" I ponder aloud.

I reach for the broom and dustpan but then let my arms fall to my sides in defeat. I glance up from the floor where Stella's distinctive pubic hair swirls around the station to look her square in the eye. We hold each other's gaze until laughter begins to erupt from each of our exhausted souls.

"We could have used the color wheel, Stella," I eek out between fits of muscle cramping laughter as tears involuntarily run down my face.

The receptionist passes by and wonders aloud, "what the hell is so funny?" - only encouraging more giggles and tears.

As she takes in the scene and the mess, her eyes widen and she focuses on Stella with disgust.

"Don't say a word and you keep your voice down. I don't want anyone to see," Stella hissed at her while wiping tears from her cheeks.

I assume a yoga squat position on the floor, unable to stand through my silent laughter convulsions. The poor receptionist reaches down offering to help me up, but quickly retracts her aid asking in horror, "wait, have you touched them?" She throws her hands up in the air, spins on her heel and walks off in disgust. "I am not sweeping up after this appointment."

Meanwhile, Gabby, who resides in the adjacent station, makes her ill-timed entrance into work. "Hi, Stella, how are you?" she cheerfully shouts to the woman trying to gain her composure. "Did you bring breakfast, what's in the bag?"

More laughter - shrieks and yelps of two women trying not to make a scene while very much making a scene.

"You don't want any of these baked goods," I manage.

At that, Stella's sense of humor and honor collide in an abrupt ending to our giggle fest as she spins in her chair and lands a fast slap to my cheek. "Enough," she says through gritted teeth.

I sober up fast. The shock of it was more memorable than the sting. Slowly, I bring my hand to my face and try to make sense of what just happened, but before I can register any emotion beyond confusion, Stella carries on with the task at hand like it is perfectly normal to fling your pubic hair all over a place of business and then slap her for making a joke out of it.

"What are you going to do with my hair today?"

At that, I snap back into my realization that something is up with Stella, "Hey, you were pretty demanding to get in today, why the rush?"

Stella explains, "I have party tomorrow and we are having everyone over right after. I want to have special hair. It is a party."

"First off, you go walking every week with these old people that don't even color their hair. They are not going to notice your party hair," I chide.

"I am the head of the club! I am kind of a big deal!" Stella touts.

I reply with, "Oh, you're kind of a big deal? Your 'deal' is floating all around my station right now. Let me sit down and think this through."

I bury my head in my hands for a very public why-me-moment. I quickly ping pong from anger to disbelief.

Why do some women think that they have to always have their natural hair color their whole lives? Dear God, we should never stay the same. Life changes. We change. The only thing we can count on is change. Embrace it!

As we get older every woman that ever walked into a hair salon has, at one point, brought a picture from a magazine, a photo of a stranger's color or cut, curtain tassels (yes, that happened), dog hair (yes, that too), and of course the personal stash of hair that has never been seen - all in the name of the perfect do.

Is there really such a thing as perfect?

The Crown

"Let your hair do the talking."

-All things Hair

"Hi, my name is Mia. Have a seat in my chair."

I become keenly aware of my height whenever a new client approaches my station. Looming over the chair, I sense the client quite literally "sizing me up". Capable. I exude capability and consciously exude confidence in place of any doubts I might secretly harbor, which are few.

It takes me a moment to situate this one in my realm of understanding. The client is in her late 40's but clearly clings to her mid 20's. She has a full face of bad makeup – eyebrows penciled in and shaped like Mr. Everest, eyeliner inching into raccoon territory, lips lined like a child's clandestine drawing on a white wall, and shriveling lips painted a full three times lighter. But, it all pales in comparison to those boobs. They are perky, fresh-water balloons proudly shouting hello from the deep V-neck blouse attempting to contain them. It was a wonder I wasn't greeted by a nipple. I briefly wondered what law of physics was bending in order to keep them in there.

The hair, though, WOWZA! Her hair is like a Q-tip top. It was swept up into a messy, glaringly bleached white bun. Upon closer look, it is the texture of cotton candy, wispy and light enough to awkwardly float on air. The pink or blue of a carnival concession could only be an improvement over the out of place wisp of cloud billowing over her head. Miracles are instore for the day, I think to myself.

This client is a referral - the friend of a friend who dated your cousin kind of referral - the big business and big paycheck kind of referral. The kind that walks in with big demands and bigger expectations and craves to be treated like royalty. Luckily, that is my forte.

With an introspective smile, I place my hands on the nebulous tuft in front of me. I begin to gently comb my fingers through the project, physically and mentally analyzing the being in my care. I meet the client's eyes and reissue my display of knowing capability. Words would only slow the settling process. The touch, the silence, and the smile are all choreographed to create a flawless aura of security and sanctuary. No words are offered, just a comforting, well placed smile. No one comes to me for something as simple and straightforward as a haircut. It is safe harbor, transformation, and magic they seek. That is what I provide.

The client in the mirror has beautiful, straight, white teeth. She sits with the erect posture of an accomplished lady. Her hands are folded in her lap, right hand over left and left leg over her right. I notice the three-inch heels and the perfectly manicured toes.

Being a hairdresser is more than just designing hair. The clients seek to be discovered. They seek the uncovering of a hidden gem. They seek aid in unfurling their butterfly's wings. A first-time client is the most challenging. I notice their attire, their posture, their confidence - or lack thereof. Body language is part of the design of the hair, how high is the chin held, how straight is the neck. But, the best part is the story. I love the telling of the story.

We all have a story, no doubt. The story tells me what type of crown is sought. Women may wear many crowns over a lifetime, often many within a year. Once the right one graces her figure, she will hold on to it for life. The color seems to be the centerpiece's jewel. Once a blond, always a blond. If they change it, inevitably, they're back in the chair saying, "Make me blonde again, I can't do it."

I rest my hands on the client's shoulders and am met with a flinch and an exclamation of, "oh, your hands are so cold!"

Slowly and gently, I withdraw them knowing this one is going to be sensitive.

I ask, "What is your name again? I apologize, the receptionist didn't tell me."

She replies with a confident air, "Lida".

"Well, Lida, I am glad to meet you and I know you were referred to me today. So, how can I help you? I hear you want a cut and color. Is that correct?" I ask.

"Yes," Lida replies with much certainty.

At that moment, my cell phone rings in the distance. Well, it doesn't ring, so much as honk. The alert has been specifically chosen to warn me as to the drama on the other end of the line. The jolt I feel at the sound of the call serves as a slight warm up for what I expect to follow.

"It sounds like it's coming from the restroom," Isabella, the receptionist, calls out without raising her head from her work.

"I guess I left it in there," I call back, "please go get it."

"Do I have to?" Isabella retorts.

"If you want to keep your job, you do," I fiercely fire back.

Evil glares are exchanged.

Isabella meanders her way toward the restroom, stooping to pick up an invisible scrap on the floor. She knows better than to involve herself in that honking. As she enters the restroom, the call clicks off and she lifts up a silent prayer. Her relief was met with the insistent ringing of the salon phone, and there was no doubt who that could be.

Isabella yells over the new alert, "I didn't make it."

I sarcastically commiserate, "I'm sure that was not on purpose."

Meanwhile, Lida shifts in the chair, silently proclaiming with wide, scared eyes, *what did I get myself into?*

Isabella lifts the salon's receiver to her ear knowing her customary greeting is not necessary. She pops her head out from the breakroom where she caught the call and says, "She wants to talk to you."

"Tell her I'm with a client," I holler.

"She's not taking no for an answer," Isabella replies with an accompanying eye roll.

I return the gesture in solidarity.

"Just take the call and get your daily dose over with early," Isabella yell-whispers with her hand over the receiver.

I exhale with all the control I can muster. With a calm and overly sweet smile, I apologize and say to Lida, "I need to get this. That's my daughter, the receptionist, if you're wondering why we're yelling at each other.

"Oh, I get it," Lida empathizes, "We all have family like that." We share a laugh in mutual understanding.

As I walk up to the front desk to take the call, one of my favorite clients enters through the front door.

"Bennie!" I belt out, "What are you doing here? You don't have an appointment, right?"

I reach for the phone with one hand and hold up a finger of the other hand indicating he should not actually answer that question yet. He leans over the desk and gestures for a kiss. I lean in and we kiss on the cheeks and Bennie then puts his hands on his heart and mouths back to me, "You just made my day".

I roll my eyes, beaming, and sit down to look at the appointment book.

"Hold on, hold on, give me a minute," I repeat as I flip through the pages. "Ok, I'll squeeze you in tomorrow. Do you still want Friday's appointment as well? Yes? Ok, just a blow dry then. Okay...okay...okay."

I roll my eyes again, meeting Bennie's gaze and mouth, "sorry". He waves his hand, "It's no big deal".

I begin to get a little feisty with the person on the phone. "Hello, I have a client in my chair, one standing at the front desk, and I don't know where Isabella is. I really need to go. See you tomorrow." I snap into the receiver.

As I hang up the phone, Bennie quickly inquires, "Do you have plans tonight?"

"Why?" I coyly reply.

"I'm singing in the bar at the Italian restaurant down the way at 8 o'clock."

"Well, I'm done here at 7. Let me see if Isabella will stay home with the kids. I'll check with Hank to see if he wants to go." I tick off the details of the necessary preparations.

Bennie interjects, "You could bring your girlfriends, too."

"Okay, okay, I gotta go," I start to walk off, turning over my shoulder to blow him a parting kiss.

Bennie shouts a friendly, "I love you."

I wink back.

Isabella recognizes the safety in returning to the front desk but meets my irritated glare on the way.

"No, I am not babysitting," she whispers under her breath as we pass.

"You owe me," I insist.

"For what?" Isabella asks incredulously.

I take my place behind the chair, returning my hands to Lida's shoulders as if the whirlwind of duties never happened. "Let's begin again," I say as much for myself as for Lida.

"Explain what you want to do today and then let's make the magic begin... Sound good?" I say with a huge smile, barely hiding the fractious stirrings I am desperately trying to put behind me. "God, I hope this turns out," I think to myself.

Lida explains that she has been doing her hair herself for years.

"No!" I say in feigned disbelief.

Lida is recently divorced and feels like she needs a change. She wonders if she should go darker. Ah, the dreaded change. I know this situation well. Women who need a change in their lives, like a new purpose, a new passion, a new awakening, usually start with their hair color.

"Here we go," I think, "I'll change her hair and then in three days, tops, she'll be back in here asking to be a blonde again."

"Great!" I declare enthusiastically, "let me get the color wheel and you can pick out your next look!"

"No, no, you're the expert, you pick the color," Lida corrects.

I strategize a color that will fulfill Lida's need for exhilaration and won't complicate my own booked schedule with a retouch in the next couple days.

In an eight-hour day in the salon, it only takes one phone call, one delayed client, one color gone wrong, one chatty client and the whole day goes to shit.

In my line of work, talent is secondary to connection. Listening, letting people be seen, and earning the client's vulnerability are the real job requirements. There aren't many that leave my chair without a kiss or a hug. I learned

14

through my yoga practice that one of the most human needs is touch. Being Italian meant it is in my blood to touch; to reach out and embrace everyone I meet. Lida will not be any different. I will hug her as we part ways. It is who I am.

At the end of the day, it is about how I care for the crown. The crown needs to leave shinier, different, and exquisite. The person in my keep must taste the exalted status of royalty. They must feel the intangible importance of my attention and adoration, as well as see in their reflection adornment and grace. A woman's crown is her identity.

Tuesdays are normally a busy day in the salon. As I continue to fix Lida's hair, the next appointment sits waiting in the front, engaging in small talk with Isabella. Isabella says the best perk of the job is talking to the clients. If they bring me gifts, which they so often do, Isabella gets first pick of the baked goods, flowers, and candy.

I yell out over my shoulder to the waiting client, "is it going to be the usual?"

"Yes, I am boring," the client admits. Thank God for a few "boring" clients, I think.

I call Isabella over and instruct her to go to the back and mix the color. "I'm running fifteen minutes behind and it will be a debacle of a day if I don't catch up somewhere."

Lida apologizes as if it were her who set me back due to her difficult requests. Lida's hair had actually been quick,

15

but had turned out wrong. I knew she would graciously claim to love her change now, but would be back within three days to lighten it up again.

I thanked Lida for coming and doted over her beauty. Lida touched her hair and thanked me for the transformation. As she stands, I grip her hands in my own and hold tight.

"Thank you for trusting me. It was such an enjoyable time together. Any questions, please call. I am here for you," I squeeze as I speak.

As I walk Lida to the front desk, I lean into Isabella and instruct her to put Lida somewhere in the next three days.

"I did already," Isabella winks.

I lean into Lida and hug her. Lida holds on tight and whispers her thanks again. As I pull back, she is crying. "Are you okay?" I ask.

"This was the best two hours I've had in a long time. I love the buzz of the salon; watching people come and go. Everyone leaves with a smile of their face. You are lucky to have this place to come to everyday," she says through a bright, tearful smile.

Tears well up in my eyes as I soak in Lida's envious observations.

"You look beautiful," I manage in lieu of thanks. "See you soon."

I turn toward my next client, arms outstretched. We embrace one another, give each other a kiss on the cheek and I ask, "How are you feeling today?"

"Better now that I'm here."

This client sits down in my chair. I place my hands warmly on this woman's shoulders, smile, and then begin to draw my fingers through her hair.

The crown is different, but the same.

A Typical Day

"You ever have those bad hair days where you just look like a troll doll?"

-The Salon Business

"Oh lord, I am late," I grumble.

First, the alarm didn't go off. Then, I spill chai tea on my shirt and the whole outfit has to be changed. Of course, the kids have perfected the art of stalling this morning in a way that can only be achieved when mom is already frantic. My youngest, Grace, needs to be taken to band practice before school and her brother, Nick, wants to tag along.

The stop light by my house is flashing red, so the line to turn right is ten cars deep. Grace and Nick argue the whole way there. As I pull through the drop off lane, Nick jumps out and yells, "See ya," over his shoulder. Grace slowly pushes open the door, then leans in to give me a kiss and thanks me before she slides out. I roll down the window and draw in a breath, readying myself to deliver my standard motherly advice, but Grace turns and shouts, "make good choices," beating me to it. I smile, repeating the family adage, "Make good choices. Go tell your brother," I add.

"He won't listen to me," Grace shrugs. We both laugh knowingly. I blow my baby girl a kiss and pull away with a "Ciao, see you at the salon later."

I glance at my reflection in the rearview mirror. "Ugh, bad hair day. I'll have to fix it at work," I whisper to myself.

As I pull up to the salon, I immediately notice something a bit off. Every single blind is completely closed. The building looks oddly shuddered and unwelcoming. Normal closing procedures would leave them half open and I am pretty sure I was the last to leave yesterday. I put my key in the lock, push the door open, and pause to look around. I take in irrelevant details of the room, waiting for some noteworthy observation or clue to cement my suspicions. As my sleuthy senses are focusing on the décor, my phone breaks the silence and sends me a foot in the air. I was not expecting a call so early. Who could it be at 7:30am? I look down; see that it is Gabby, my girlfriend and coworker.

Gabby regularly calls at odd hours, but not the "odd hours" before noon. I answer and blithely bid my friend, "good morning, what has you up so early?"

"Oh, I couldn't sleep. What time are you thinking about getting to the salon this morning?" Gabby fishes.

"Already here," I announce.

"Why!?" Gabby shouts back.

I explain, "I had to drop Grace off at band practice and I thought I'd just come in and clean up a bit since I left in a rush last night to get to Tony's singing gig."

"Oh," Gabby curtly replies.

"What's up with you?" I ask.

"Nothing. I'll see you soon. I have a 9am. Okay. Okay," Gabby replies hastily.

I put the phone down in my station and resume my scan of the salon. I note takeout food in the trash, the bathroom light is on, and the break room has candy wrappers scattered across the table. Someone definitely came in last night, I conclude.

I move through the salon, opening up the blinds, letting the light pour in. I empty the trash (again). I turn unneeded lights back off and then enter the massage room. My intuition is flickering on. I stand there, evaluating the room. The massage therapist was not in yesterday, yet there are sheets in the laundry basket. There are candy wrappers all over this room, too. That's weird, I think. Why is someone having a party in here? As I turn to walk out, I notice a bracelet on the floor. I stoop to pick it up and immediately recognize it (and all this other handy work) as Gabby's. "What the hell?!" I shout to no one.

Again, my phone rings. It's my other friend, Dani. "Good morning," I answer, not even trying to hide my dismay.

Dani begins, "I just saw Nick at school. He said you dropped Grace and him off early today."

"Yes," I offer absentmindedly, still piecing together the mystery in front of me.

Dani clamors on, "Are we still on for happy hour Friday night? Let's go at 4:00 and the rest of the girls can meet us at 5:00…"

"Dani," I interrupt, "I think Gabby brought someone here to the salon last night and had a sex fest in the massage room."

"Oh, I'm sure she did," Dani replies matter-of-factly.

"Why would you think that?" I press.

"Hello! She lives with her parents and those two kids. I am pretty sure she can't take anyone home with her. The salon's pretty much her only option," Dani explains flatly.

"She's not even dating anyone," I rationalize.

"Hello!" Dani repeats emphatically, "Do you need to date them to ride the pony?"

"Okay, now I am grossed out. She got her love juices all over the massage table! There's crap everywhere!" I shout into the phone in a horrified and slightly amused tone.

"Oh, she got it on in there, all right. But, with who?" Dani asks, now fully engrossed in the gossip. "It could be anyone. She has a crush on a handful of men and most of them are married."

"Maybe it's the married one from the gym," I speculate.

Dani cuts off our fun, "I have to go, I'm walking into work. Wear gloves when you clean that table. Maybe we'll get her drunk enough that she fesses up Friday night at happy hour."

"Oh, I'll get it out of her before Friday night," I assure her.

9:00am rolls around and in strolls Gabby. Her client has been waiting fifteen minutes already. Gabby looks hung over and guilty and her hair is bad. Wait, what? Dear God, she gave herself bangs; too short bangs.

"Good morning, Gabby. You look different this morning. Bangs, I see. And you seem to have a skip in your step. Did you have a good night last night?" I whip around to look her in the eyes.

"I know you know," she mumbles.

"I don't know the half of it… Yet," I reply under my breath while searing her with my glare.

Gabby waves me off and heads to the break room.

Isabella sashays after Gabby, giddily singing, "I'm getting the scoop!"

Soon I can hear Gabby and Isabella in the breakroom laughing their asses off. Gabby's client is steaming alone in her chair. My client is craning her ear toward the gossip, itching to know the details.

A phone call interrupts my eavesdropping, as my boyfriend, Hank, calls and I excuse myself to relay an earful of juicy sex fest details.

Surprisingly, my mother, Bea pipes up from the waiting area, "Did you say sex fest in the massage room?"

At which point, the UPS guy yells from the corner, "Count me in!"

Isabella innocently reenters the room and responds to the UPS guy's comment with, "I want to do whatever he's in on."

I place an irrelevant hand over the phone receiver as my client and I collapse in a roar of laughter. Hank gives up and hangs up after he realizes the giggles are not stopping anytime soon.

Gabby finally emerges from the break room to find my client and me red faced and wiping away tears, Isabella drooling over the UPS guy, my mom sporting a look of disgust, and her bracelet taped at eye level to her mirror sending the undeniable message that her boss knows exactly what she did last night.

"But who had sex in the massage room? I need to know," my client exclaims.

Gabby whips her head around to meet my glare. I lock eyes with her and slowly raise my finger and point directly at her, holding the pose until the intensity becomes a solid existence between us. The whole salon engages, slowly transitioning from gasping for breath between fits of laughter to absolute stillness. A few tears from the recent chortling still drip down cheeks as they all wait, unblinking, for the tension to snap.

Cue the UPS guy, "I'm still in if anyone cares," initiating a cascade of ladies eager to take him up on his offer (or break silence).

My mother crowns the moment with a confused, but energetic, "well, I guess I'm in too!" She accepts the laughter, and adds, "but, I thought we were talking about someone having sex in the massage room."

The thing about friendship is that you love the person - the whole person - despite and because of their actions. And when you come to know them so well that you don't require an explanation for their affairs; you can simply accept that things were done, then the ability to let live and revel in the story over a happy hour when they're ready to tell it becomes the fulfilling thing of camaraderie.

But secrets are alluring, and everyone wants in. I want in, my client, my mom, the UPS man, the new receptionist - but today no one gets the truth out of Gabby. It's her secret to contend with and when she comes to terms with it, I'll be there to laugh with her. I just hope her bangs grow out before then, so I don't have to laugh at her a little.

Life– is all in the hair. When women change their hair, it is a sign of needing a change or attention or maybe a cry for excitement. It's when they enact that desperation on themselves without the help of my professional services that they regret the change.

Hair and scissors are not friends when you're in low places.

The Old Versus the Young

"Messy hair, thirsty hearts."

-*The Brunette Travel*

I control this space. It's mine and I am happy here. Everything has its place and I decide what that place is. I am my own master and I have mastered my trade. I am a woman with purpose and talent and charisma. I worked hard to get here. Each lesson is stacked in the corner of my mind and I dance through my days with those lessons informing, but not weighing me down. There is lightness in my love for the work and a tether of maturity that makes me good, really well at this. I own this space in so many profound ways. It is here that I am my most accomplished. My space, my creation, my life, my salon – until my mother sits down in the chair at the center.

"You look tired, baby," she'd denounce loud enough for all my employees to hear.

"Are you behind on laundry? Why else would you wear those together?" she'd observe of my wardrobe in front of waiting clients.

My mother was a weekly event, yes event. She never hesitated to resume her parenting as if I was a schoolgirl, still occasionally putting my shirt of backwards or only brushing the front of my hair. She nitpicked whatever was out of place on me without abandon as if I was her space of control.

She was the worst about telling me how to do my job. She critiqued my every brush stroke - too much spray, too much heat, too much curl. It really was all too much. When she walked in the salon it was all about her.

How do you manage your mother in your place of business? Let me tell you, you don't. My mother is full blood Italian - Sicilian on top of it. I don't think she has a filter. Whatever is on her mind is interjected into the world. Oh, she didn't care who heard it either. She was the elder and I was the child, no matter how much I thought of myself as an accomplished, adult woman.

My mother wanted the prime time of the week - Friday mornings at 9:00 am. This was a big request since she never paid me, and tips were only offered if she won in bingo that week.

Loretta wanted to come in on Friday at the same time because she had bunco at 11:00. She wanted her hair done for that game every week. She is the sweetest lady I've ever met. She brought me food and gifts and complimented my every move. She gushed over my outfits, she adored my cuts and colors, and she praised my youthful glow. Every visit was homage to my autonomy, and she paid.

My loyalties were being tested - my mother and her condescending, unpaying, thankless spot or me and my self-respect, income, and general badass-ness, in the form of Loretta – who gets the coveted 9am Friday spot? It seems like it should be an easy decision, right? It is hard to say no to your mother, though. And it is hard to put yourself first – over anyone.

Loretta got the spot. If she was getting a color, I would squeeze my mother in while Loretta sat with color on her head. My mother felt that squeeze and she never liked it. I had made up my mind that I would choose myself first. I love my mother and I can see that it was hard for her to recognize the gravity of my decision since "I" was sitting in the form of Loretta's good hair. But, we made it work. It only took two years. Somewhere along the way, my mother finally softened to Loretta and we became a happy family, enjoying our 9am Friday throne.

The dynamic of two wise older women imparting knowledge on the young sassy one imprinted me. They were as different as night and day, oil and water, and they both had profound things to say about family, food, and grandkids. When they turned on each other and offered unwelcome advice, their true colors came out. Loretta, the water – fluid and forgiving. My mom, the oil – smooth and driven. There is so much value in the clear confidence of wise women, mostly, that there is not one way to be a badass.

Many Hats

"My hairstyle is called, I tried."

-Unknown

I wear so many hats. I start my day off as a divorced woman - that hat is one I just wake up wearing. Soon, my kids force me into my next role, "The Mom". By the time I leave the house, I don the hats of hairdresser, salon owner, counselor, therapist, repair worker, custodian, taxi driver, chef, girlfriend, sister, daughter, and yoga student.

I love each of the roles, but I feel I am pulled in a hundred different directions at once. My very being is getting worn down by the constant shifting and dancing and catering to the requirements of each interaction.

I average ten hours per day at the salon. I could have ten, even fifteen clients. Fifteen personalities. Fifteen different stories. Each one requires a different hat.

The diversity of people through those doors makes my head spin. Everyone had a hot opinion about something and I was all people pleaser back then.

I could not admit to most clients that I practiced yoga. I had a few that thought it was literally the devil's exercise. I never spoke up for myself or my new passion. I kept quiet and grinned through their ranting and raving about how awful they thought yoga is.

The "many hats" I wore meant that I became one with the client, in that I fused with them and found a way to be completely in agreement with everything they said. I allowed them to be utterly themselves at the expense of me being me. Little by little, I sacrificed my soul to be the person my client needed. It was my living and my business and I was ready to preserve it in any way I had to.

I learned a lot by giving up so much of myself. I stand for what I believe in now, and I don't wear hats like that anymore. I have one hat... Mia's Hat.

Sometimes I hated myself after work because of the lies. I would lie about God, politics, women's choices. I watched other hairdressers speak up on their views and they lost clients. I couldn't afford that, so I agreed with most everyone that came into my chair. But, when you are a single woman with three kids and in survival mode, you don't have the luxury of fucking up your job because of an opinion. What did it really matter at the end of the day? Would it make a difference? No... It wouldn't (other than where they got their hair done).

I had many clients that I could be myself around. We were on the same page about everything - life, career, politics, kids, men, and friends, all of it. No fancy hats with them, just pure love and pure fun.

I guess, looking back, that was the joy hat. I love that hat and those folks. They were the ones that got a hug, laughs, and I shared stories about my life and parents. There was trust and camaraderie. I knew they loved me and much as I loved them.

Truth sometimes is ugly, but there is always some beauty in truth - for truth's sake. I stand in what I believe now and I don't wear hats that don't allow me to be authentic. I do love a good sun hat!

Wall to Wall Carpet

"Whenever you're feeling powerless just remember one

thing....

A single one of your pubic hairs can shut down an entire

restaurant."

-Dump a Day

There is energy to the salon today. It is vibrating here. It is less like the purr of a content cat and more like the buzz of an angry beehive, though. Smiles are replaced with scowls, hurried shuffles replaced with stomps, the clitter-clatter of utensils on tables sounds like they're all being thrown in metal pans. I'm feeling a bit salty myself. Every client has been late with a wild excuse. The full moon is making its presence known.

I have been two steps behind all day. With only a few clients left, I yearn for the end of this disaster.

Right now, is fine, though. I am catching my breath and slowing down. I love blow-drying hair. It's like a moving meditation. I never talk, I just melt into the rhythmic motion and the consistent sound. I realign my bearings during this time. Except, this time my client is not having it. She is shifting in her seat and grumbling under the sound of the dryer.

"I have to get my kids, could you hurry?" she snaps with feigned sweetness.

I silently smile and nod and picture the glass of wine awaiting me at the end of this day. I am so close.

"Your new client has been waiting 20 minutes," Isabella barks, ripping me out of my dreamy aura.

"Why didn't you tell me earlier?" I bark back.

"You know you're running behind," she defends with arms outstretched and palms upturned.

"Two minutes," I say curtly.

I see my client out and slink up to the front desk. "What are we doing?" I ask Isabella in regards to the new client who is obviously anxious, kneading her hands in the waiting area.

"Wax."

Well, this won't do. "WTF, why would you give it to me?" I whisper in Isabella's ear.

"It's her first time and she said she wants the owner," Isabella offers, knitting her eyebrows together.

"I don't see how the hell that has anything to do with it," I whisper-exclaim, raising my hands over my head, but crouching down in a failed effort to maintain a semblance of composure.

I walk toward my awaiting wax job. She is striking. Her features are angelic and her hair is soft and light. She smiles sheepishly as she stands and I take in an imposing woman of immense stature and girth. I realize I didn't get her name, but I'm flustered now and rationalize I'll just knock this eyebrow wax out in no time and move along to my glass of wine.

"Let's get a look at those eyebrows, shall we? Have you ever had them waxed before?" I blithely ask as we enter the aesthetician's room.

She looks at me confused, raises her perfectly manicured eyebrows, and cocks her head to the side.

"Oh shit," I prepare myself.

"I'm here for a bikini wax."

I would like to say I responded without missing a beat, but I did, in fact, miss a beat. Then, "Bikini wax it is," I manage through an obviously forced smile. I turn my back, lift my chin, massage both sides of my neck, try to roll out the worsening tension, and take a deep breath.

I turn, handing her a towel and instruct her to leave her underwear on and just place the towel between her legs. "I'll be back in a minute."

I walk out of the room and close the door behind me. Leaning against the wall, I close my eyes and start a mantra, "I can wax with ease, I can wax with ease, I can wax with ease." I start to feel it. I start to believe it. Slowly, I open my eyes, ready to take this on. Isabella is standing right in front of me, nose to nose.

"Oh shit," I say again, this time out loud. Then, "You are a dumb ass. It's a bikini wax."

"I know."

I flip her off as she walks away laughing.

I muster my will to go on and reenter the room. The nameless client is laying there on her back, with her knees daringly spread wide like she is in a yoga class, and the pitiful little towel is doing its best to cover the curled-up bear cub that surely was sleeping on top of her crotch.

I catch and hide the look of horror that flashes over my face just as she raises her head and pops those damn eyebrows right up and over the fluffy animal between us.

"Have you ever had a bikini wax before?" I say as the first bead of sweat forms over my upper lip.

"Never," she replies then launches into a nervous rambling account of her boyfriend's request for this.

I catch a third of it, but am honestly, preoccupied by the sheer breadth of coverage and unnatural length of these pubes in front of my face.

"Can you excuse me for one minute?" I am not prepared.

The client nods.

I dash out of the room and grab my clippers, scissors, and comb from my station. Isabella and the other girls look on as I move like lightning.

"What are you doing in there? Giving a haircut to a chonch?" someone yells.

I stop in mid dart, "yes."

Everyone stifles laughter. Just then, I see my next client through the window parking her car. Sweat starts to bead up on my forehead. Please let this day end.

I steel myself at the door. As I enter, the client seems a bit thrown off by all the tools in my hand. I professionally explain that waxing works best with a specific length of hair and (straight face, Mia) hers is a bit longer than ideal.

Now emboldened by the utterance of "pubic hair," the client proceeds to reveal to me that her boyfriend wants more than a bikini wax.

"All of it," she says sheepishly.

"All of it," I repeat pursing my lips to avoid the look of utter horror wanting to form on my face.

At that, the client whips off the towel to reveal "all of it" and the look of horror finds itself a home on my face. There, in front of me, is a vision I cannot unsee. Wall to wall carpet on a woman! I jump back, steadying myself on the cart behind me. I inhale sharply for the last time that hour.

"Yes, yes, yes," I squeak, forcing a smile. You're a professional, Mia, I coach myself. Pull it together.

I start with a little scissor over comb but quickly move to the big guns. The clippers are sitting beside me and I reach for them in disbelief. I stare at the buzzing contraption in my hand then glance back to the carpet I'm about trim. This is the worst. The client is talking but I'm not registering her words over the sound of the clippers and the focus required to tame this wild animal.

I can't help but think of the things she must get caught up in here.

I finish trimming the fur coat stretching from just under her belly button and running down her inner thighs almost to her knees. I can feel the beads of sweat tickling my forehead and the sweat soaking through my shirt as I wipe them away with the sleeve of my upper arm.

"Can I ask you for a favor?" the client asks as I finish up sheering her vag. I almost choke on my spit.

"My boyfriend wants all of the hair gone."

"I know, a Brazilian," I confirm.

"Well, I need more," she says matter of factly.

I stop what I'm doing. She could not want what I think she wants. "More?"

"More" she says as she picks up her leg, points, and says "butthole too."

In my head, I'm thinking a mile a minute – what the hell? What the fuck? I want to go home. Shit, shit, shit.

The sweat is dripping from my forehead now, down my temples, into eyes.

I bite my lip and smear the sticky wax onto the hair covering the client's hip bone, pressing hard to pull the skin and not just the hair in the direction of the swipe. Then I lay the strip, apply pressure along the length, smoothing the fabric to her body, and rip. She inhales sharply. I repeat, one after another, fast and furious. The client's knuckles are white as she grips the sides of the table. Her toes are curled under. Her face is contorted. Her breathing is shallow. Her whole body is clammy.

I keep applying and ripping as fast I can. At that moment, I feel time stop. The miserable, less-hairy, more-sticky client lifts her leg up into the air and reveals to me all of her womanhood. Chicken is all I can think. Come on, it looks like chicken, and it is right in my face. I have never seen another woman's chicken before. Sweat is pouring out between my boobs, soaking through my shirt.

"Every hair," the client instructs.

I am in that chicken now, pulling it, stretching it. The lips are flapping every time I pull a wax strip. The whole of her crotch area is starting to swell slightly.

There's a knock at the door. I use my sleeve to mop the sweat from my face and open it slightly. It's Isabella asking if she needs to reschedule my next appointment, but when she focuses and takes in my state, she reflexively and dramatically gags. Wax and pubic hair are everywhere.

"Yes, please reschedule. I'm going to be a while longer," I say with a cheerful voice, but a pained expression while trying to hide my hands behind the door.

"You have pubic hair on your face," Isabella says plainly as if it was the most perfectly normal thing to say to your mom at work, then she pivots on her heel and walks away.

I dive back in. Rip. Flap. Rip. Flap. I remind myself that I am never eating chicken again. I allow myself the complete formalized thought that I do not like the smell of pussy. But, I'm getting close to the end now – to be interpreted positively and negatively.

I pause for a moment and search for the best way to access the grand finale. I'm a hairdresser. I waxed one eyebrow in school. I don't really have a plan for this butthole.

Just then, the client kicks both legs up the air, rolls her pelvis back, and lays still. Waiting.

Okay, we're doing this, I think and dive back in. The smell of her chonch is making me dizzy. One hand is holding this woman's lips open and other one is painting her butthole. I am not enjoying this. I can see the man in the boat. He's right there between her lips, ready to jump ship. Oh, dear God, I need to breathe. I am holding my breath. I am never going to get the smell out of my nose.

Meanwhile, the client is relaxing her head back, staring vacantly at the ceiling. She's calm, even serene, comfortable in her nakedness.

My back is killing me. I am soaked through with sweat. There is pubic hair all over the room. I need a break.

I come up for air and ask, "Do you mind if I grab my water from my station? Just a sec."

"I could use a minute myself," the client grants, lowering her legs and closing her knees.

As I exit the room, every head in the salon turns and silence ensues. I pull the door shut, fold my hands behind my back, close my eyes and stand still for full minute. I am fully aware of my audience but am unable to face them and unable to avoid them, so I close my eyes and breath.

When I'm as ready as I'll ever be, I flicker my eyelids open, focus on my station, and slowly walk toward it. I reach out for my water bottle and yell, "ahhhhh" at the sight of my pubic hair covered fingers.

Isabella fake vomits again. Gabby throws her head back and laughs out loud. Two other employees snicker, trying to hide their amusement. Every client is staring at me with wide eyes.

"Not a word!" I hiss, wagging my finger at them all.

Isabella walks over to me, looks me over and says, "Your mascara is smeared, you have sweat bubbles on your top lip, and you have a wax strip full of pubic hair stuck to your shoe. Are you done?"

I take a huge gulp of water and begin to walk back to the room shaking my head no.

From my station, Isabella yells, "your client rescheduled and ran across the street and got you this." She holds up my favorite Pinot Noir. "She knows you well and knows you're going to need this after today."

I return to the room with my head sagging and my arms swinging like a defeated toddler.

I return to find the client (whose name I really should know since I know the rest of her so well) hastily getting off the phone with her boyfriend.

As I cut a few more strips of paper to complete the job, I am thinking how much I want to kill this boyfriend and how I can't blame him for wanting all of this gone.

I start calculating the price tag for this full haircut, clipper cut, wax, my fingers in her chonch and vow that she is not getting out of here cheap.

"Okay, final place. Are you ready?" I ask, while wondering the same of myself.

The client closes her eyes, crosses her arms, and lifts her legs. I bend over, adjust the towel over the chicken, making sure the butthole is still exposed. I slap wax on both sides, center one paper strip over both, rip with all my might, repeat top and bottom, come up for air, and announce that I am done.

"Thank God," the client calls out throwing her arms over her head.

"Thank God," I concur. "You and me both."

"It was a pleasure getting to know you," I lie. "Good luck with your new boyfriend. Excuse me, I have to get going. Isabella will check you out."

I hastily walk out of the room and pause outside the door once again. Did that really just happen? I take a deep breath of clean, fresh air. I feel like a sailor rejoicing as he reaches land. I survived. I am on the other side of that event.

I make a beeline for the bathroom. I become aware of the dampness of my entire top as I move through the cooler air. Once hidden safely inside, I start to process the whole event

– only to be interrupted as Isabella steps inside and stares at me. We say nothing.

She watches me as I frantically begin to swat at the pubic hair on my shoes. I let out a little growl of frustration and start brushing off my cape, then start picking at the ones stuck to my fingers. I lean toward the mirror and gasp in horror at the pubic hair stuck to my top lip.

Isabella just looks on in silence.

I frantically wash my hands and face until not really feeling clean, but satisfied at the lack of visible evidence.

I whip my wet face toward Isabella, ready to unleash all my pent-up aggression, but she beats me to it, "I am so sorry. I will never make that mistake again."

I choose to hammer this lesson in. "You will never schedule me another bikini wax. Ever. Never again."

"Okay," she says with the humility of a scolded puppy.

"Never." I am still too angry to let her off the hook.

"It's like I had sex with that woman and did not enjoy it," My eyebrows were furled at the beginning of the sentence. My hands were clenched. By the end, I cracked. The utter ridiculousness of the statement and the day got to me and I was unable to contain a grin. Soon, the grin creeped into a giggle. The giggle evolved into uncontrollable laughter. The laughter produced tears of (mostly) joy. The episode was interrupted by a knock at the door. We carry on, ignoring it, until it grows too loud to ignore.

Isabella unlocks and slightly pushes open the door. Stella, my regular client who does not have an appointment today, is standing expectantly outside the door.

Oblivious to the moment we're having, she launches into her demand, "Honey, I'm going to need you to squeeze me in. I have a funeral tomorrow and I will see a lot of people there."

Isabella pokes her head out and surprises Stella. "Oh, I thought Mia was in there," she says.

"She is."

"Then why are you in there too?" Stella's hands are on her hips now.

"Why can't you wait until we're out?" Isabella snaps back pushing the door closed again.

The knocking resumes. Isabella is wiping pubic hair off my clothes. I sit on the toilet crying real tears now. I can't take anymore.

"Call the girls and see if they can meet at my house tonight. Tell them I'll supply the wine." I instruct Isabella through my hands as they cradle my face, supporting my head, elbows resting on knees. "And tell Stella 'No.' Give her no explanation."

My phone begins to ring from Isabella's pocket. Isabella pulls it out, glances at the screen and announces, "Its Hank. He called an hour ago and I told him you were with a client."

I extend one hand without adjusting my posture of defeat. With face still buried, I offer a, "hmm."

"Hey, I'm craving Mexican food. You want to go out for chicken tacos tonight? I know you love them!" I recall the last hour and gag a little. I start to laugh again. This time an unhinged, scary laugh of a woman on the edge. Hank is so confused.

"Bad day?" He guesses.

"I think I'm drinking my dinner tonight," I say. "I already invited the girls over for drinks."

"Have them come to the restaurant. It's on me," Hank insists.

Isabella leans in and whispers, "Can I come?"

I emphatically shake my head no. "You are babysitting because of your fuck up today."

"Uh oh! She did it again!" Hank snickers.

Isabella hugs me. Then she walks out of the bathroom, pushes past Stella who is still standing there awaiting her attention, and says over her shoulder, "Mia's not feeling well."

Stella moseys over to Gabby's station and manages to work herself in.

Just like that, one experience can change your whole view on something you love. Chicken tacos are now a thing of the past. I think I will be vegan starting today.

Thumbs Up

"If all else fails, make the hair bigger."

-Unknown

The sacred space of the salon allows women a whole existence somehow void of masculinity, yet simultaneously imbued in men. It is magical to see and feel the chemistry of community when everyone gets it. Women can be a different version of themselves in the safety of the feminine spirit. And what do we do in that warm, effervescent cocoon of womanly bonding? We talk about penises.

When given the freedom only experienced in true sanctuary, women range from worshipping their man like he is the sun and the moon to viciously slaying his existence, leaving his most shameful failures sprawled and displayed for all to judge. The stories are full of voracious longing and scornful hatred. It's great.

But, not as great as the single ladies' stories.

The single women bring the sex. They are stories of untamed, adventurous no pants dances for pure entertainment, like a restaurant review, product assessment, and a vacation recap all rolled into one.

"So how is the …. *wide eyes and gesturing hands*?" Some more curt clients would say "sex" and some would blushingly euphemize, "you know…the playground?"

48

It was me. I was the single lady who brought the sex stories.

I was a busy woman with impeccable standards and no time or patience for something that didn't make the earth shake. I was ruthless toward the boring and gregarious when it was done well. I was happy to let my clients experience my passionate romances and weigh in on my smut.

A certain on-again, off-again boyfriend with a towering physique of broad shoulders, big feet, capable hands, and yes, a big ole' love muscle, set a theory in motion that guided many interactions during that time.

"Your thumb is the same shape as your captain," I blurted.

He laughed too hard to not have already recognized it. "What do you mean?" He coyly asked.

From that day forward I asked every woman I knew to contribute to my survey. "Hey, do me a favor and compare your husband's thumb and his member." I scientifically insisted, "It has to be hard to get the best description." It was the talk of the salon. Some women thought I was crazy and some thought I was appalling. It was a great survey and it turned out I was right. Most men's thumb was shaped like his johnson. So, it began.

Salon culture shifted from hugs and open palmed waves to bid clients farewell to, you guessed it, a thumbs up for the men. "Do you like your hair, sweety? I'd ask extending my arm high and my thumb higher. They would return the gesture without fail. It was too easy. They innocently displayed their secret to a room full of intrigued observers. Enthusiastic "ohhhs" and pursed lipped "mmms" were not in response to their clean cuts.

"If we only knew what"? I heard behind me one afternoon. I stood bolt upright and smiled at my next male client. He surprised the gossip circle and overheard the group laughing about our discussion concerning the last poor guy.

Big, embarrassed, cackling laughs responded to his question. "You don't want to know, trust me. It's just girl talk (and it's not G rated)". I answered, trying to keep it classy.

In my defense, it was fresh on my mind, so, as I started shampooing him, I very discretely peered down at his hands. He caught me.

"What are looking at?"

"Nothing," I lied.

"You were checking out my hands."

"Was I?" I feinted. It didn't work. He continued to eye me accusingly. "I can't tell you. Just forget it. Please, let's just drop it."

He wouldn't. "I won't tell anyone," he promised.

I kept washing his hair thinking about how unprofessional this conversation was about to get.

"Come on," I say, ushering him to my station. I start cutting his hair. The silence is deafening.

"It must be juicy because you tell me everything," he said.

Laughter burst through my attempts at a calm and professional demeanor. "You said juicy!"

"Ok, prepare to be offended," I said, then launched into it. "Give me a thumbs up."

He displays the gesture. The hairdresser next to me notices and directs her attention to the big reveal. We knowingly smile at each other as we both surely are envisioning a crowd offering a standing ovation, a perfect 10 from all judges, a nod from a regal queen, coins spewing from a slot machine.

She winks at me and I give her a nod.

"What does it mean?" he shrieks, childishly shaking his thumbs in the air.

"Oh, you'll probably like it, thank God," I whisper as an aside.

"Thank God for what?" He asks incredulously.

I reply, "Well thank God your thumb is big and beautiful. Otherwise, it would be very hard to tell you. Ok, I feel a little dirty saying this."

He starts to laugh, "dirty?"

"Yes. I feel like I just opened the door to your amusement park," I hinted.

"What? Amusement park?" He is legitimately confused. I try again.

"You know, your play area," I steel myself against pointing to his crotch.

"My play area..." he shakes his head, "just say it."

I lean in close. But not too close, "the shape of a man's thumb is the shape of his you know – dipstick."

"Dipstick!" His eyes widen as he finally gets it. "Is that what you call it?"

"Well, not all the time. I usually referred to it as the captain or general," I say raising my chin just enough to express pride over defensiveness.

He let out an exuberant laugh that radiated the confidence of a man recently complemented on his penis proportions.

I hang my head hoping to conceal the fifty shades of red I have flushed.

"I'm not going to talk to you about my man's captain and how he steers his ship!" I say wholly embracing the nautical theme.

"Ok, ok, well, what do you think?" He chuckles as he enticingly gesticulates.

I laugh out loud. The hairdresser next to me laughs out loud. She pipes up, "you free tonight?"

"I could be for either of you," he replies with a wink.

"Enough!" I shout waiving my hands as if I could erase this situation like a white board. We all force some soothing, lengthy exhales in an attempt to gather ourselves, smirks still bubbling up from time to time.

I wrap up his haircut and attempt to bid him farewell as quickly as possible. If I could have just disappeared, I would have. As he walks out of the salon he boisterously announces, "Ladies" with both thumbs in the air. He is met with dumfounded silence, mouths ajar. So, he takes a catwalk worthy twirl and adds, "Get the word out!"

Oh, the howls.

It's My Day

"Hair doesn't make the woman, but good hair definitely

helps."

- Unknown

Weddings stress me out. It is, arguably, the most important hair day ever! I do not want to carry the notoriety of jacking up someone's big day.

This particular wedding is a really big deal. I am doing everyone's hair in the wedding and then, I get to stand next to them. My sister and my youngest daughter and I are all in the wedding. Let's just say it is a family affair.

The bride is a bit controlling. Some girls have looked forward to this day their whole life. They have planned it down to the hairpin. A good bridesmaid just goes with the flow. So, I am going with the flow.

The three words I think I heard over and over and over during the course of the six-month period leading up to the wedding were: "It's my day". This is not my first wedding. I have lived the behind the scenes prep work to transform a girl into a princess for her big day. Many times. I was trying to give her suggestions with the hair do's, what time they should be at the salon, when to arrive at the church, etc. But, it was never received well.

In all of the dozens of brides' and bridal groups' hair I have done up over my years, I have perfected the ambiance. I have champagne and orange juice waiting and breakfast brought in. This bride is not interested in my extras.

It was the day of the wedding, a fall day in October. In Phoenix, a fall day is still in the upper 90's and heat and sweat will do a number on an updo. I stressed about the whole wedding party's hair melting in the Phoenix sun in front of the bride's whole family and all of her friends. I did not want to have to stand there and observe my creations melting like candles. Especially since everyone could turn and point out that it was all my fault, while I stood there melting too.

I am a professional, though. I am ready for this. I get into the salon extra early. I was told by the bride that there would be no alcohol. I suggested I can have breakfast for everyone at the salon and she said her family is going out for breakfast, so no need. I was informed that my family had to get their hair done first because her best friend and cousin didn't want to come in too early.

I started on my sister at 8:00 am. Now, the wedding is at 2:00 pm, we had pictures at 12:30 pm, and it was a 45 minute drive to the church from the salon. I had to get my mother, my two daughters, my sister and my niece done before the rest of the bridal party arrived. My girlfriend Gabby helped out with some heads.

The bride and her entourage rolled up in a limo with a bottle of champagne in each hand as they giggled and doted over each other in the parking lot, ambling in after some time, despite being exquisitely late. I guess the "no drinking" applied to me.

I barked out, "You're late! You're going to be late for your wedding."

The bride didn't like that comment. She replied with, "you better get moving and don't piss me off on MY DAY".

I didn't say a word. I told Gabby "you take one and I will take one and let's get curling".

The tension was thick between the whole party. The bride separated us from everything. She didn't invite us to drive in the limo and we had to find our own ride to the church. I feel I should mention that I didn't charge anyone for doing their hair. It was a gift from me, a very generous gift it was turning out to be.

Silence is not my forte but today I was queen at it. I stifled every caddy remark that the bride most definitely deserved. There were so many zingers I had to let go to waste to keep the peace. Oh, it was hard. I just focused on this

French twist like no tomorrow. I was determined not to be the reason she was late to the church.

The bride noticed there were bagels and cream cheese sitting out at the station next to me. She whipped the chair around and said, "I told you we don't want to eat."

I spun the chair around so fast I think I snapped her neck. I looked her square in the eye and said, "Do you see these other people here that are in the wedding? They needed to be fed. Those are for them."

She rolled her eyes.

It was that moment that I thought maybe I won't put all the hair pins in her hair so her hair will fall apart and as if to solidify my need for vengeance, she says once again, "it's my day and make sure my hair looks good."

Silence on my end. I look over to my kids and my sister and they all roll their eyes. I begin to get hot. I feel sweat bubbles on my top lip, my pits start to get hot and I feel sweat building between my boobs. All I can think about is that puffy big sleeved dress that weighs 100 lbs. and I am already hot and its 100 degrees outside. I'm heating up from the inside and the outside.

What a day it will be.

Gabby was helping with makeup and the other bridesmaid asked if they could use the salon's makeup to finish their faces. I said, "yes" and under my breath, "sure I can keep giving. Take whatever you want. You are special and all."

It is exactly 11:45 am. I have all-hands-on-deck helping me with curling and handing me pins for the hairdos. There is a frantic and desperate buzz to the place.

I had started my own hair before everyone got there so all I needed was Gabby to pull it up, pin the shit out of it and spray the hell out of it and off we went. But, I knew we would be late. I sent the bride and her favored group off to their limo to get on the road and told her I would be late.

She yells, "You'd better not be late!"

I said, "I will be because I have to finish me."

She stormed out with her entourage and everyone else kicked it into gear.

We get the church. I use the bathroom. Everyone else goes right the alter. I can hear the bride asking about me. I run down the aisle at 12:52 pm, shouting, "here I am!"

The bride casually brushes us aside, saying "the photographer is running late, so go sit down over to the side". As we sit to the side, we settle in while wiping sweat and calming ourselves from the frantic rush to get to the church on time. Now I am fuming. They are running late?

We could have taken more time. I chide under my breath, "*it's my day*" ugh. I'm sweating again.

My sister hands me these three sticks with a single flower in the middle. "What the hell is this?" I ask.

She smirks as she shrugs and pushes this ugly thing into my hands. This is what we are carrying down the aisle? Then I looked up at the alter to see the bride posed with her best friend and cousin, barely able to hold massive and colorful bouquets fit for a queen. Finally, she calls us up to the alter with our single flowers to take three pictures and we are done. My sister and I impulsively squawk, "that's it?" We busted our butts to get here for this?

I shake my head and sass, "I have to sit down, these sticks are too heavy." My sister stifles a laugh as we move away.

The wedding begins right on time. We promenade down the aisle, looking fabulous and pretending to be sublimely happy for the lovely couple. I arrive at my perch in front of the well-dressed crowd as my stomach begins to start making very unladylike noises. "Oh dear," I thought as the realization overtook me. I began to squeeze my butt cheeks in an effort to contain the fart. I glance over at my sister and I give her an "uh oh" look, that she silently returns with a "what is going on" look. And then it slips, the fart slips out, like a squeak toy. My eyes get big, the other bridesmaids look at me with shock and dismay. I start to laugh, my sister starts to laugh, we cup our mouths and contain the cackles as best we can. We're both silently shaking in front of the entire church. I try to stop. I just can't. I can hardly breathe. The bride looks over and gives us the stink eye at which point, tears spring from my eyes and roll down my face. My silent shake laugh is threatening to erupt as a huge snort. My sister grips my leg for support which only refuels the good humor. In the nick of time, the priest graciously asks us all to be seated so my sister and I move to the nearby pew. Unluckily, I can see the groom's face from my new angle. He clearly knows something is going on and smiles knowingly. The bride doesn't approve of his friendliness.

I lean over to my sister and say, "everyone can see her nasty faces, right?" She whispers back, "hell yes."

Finally, the knot is tied. We usher out of the church and into the limo to kill two hours before the reception starts. Miraculously, my sister and I are allowed in the party cruise and are now allowed to drink, so boy do we ever.

Once the reception gets rolling, my friends who are stuck at a random table in the back and I get the innocent idea to switch their seats up near me. What could it hurt? We asked two at the "family and friends" table to swap out and they happily oblige. I am finally relaxing and enjoying the music and fanciness. The room is lively and most everyone's hair is divine.

The food is served and as everyone sits and dines, the bride notices the hair out of place. "What are your friends doing at this table" she asks with a champaign glass in her hand and a vein in her forehead.

"I just switched seats with the couple we didn't know. They are sitting back there with other people they don't know now," I logically explain.

She starts to cuss, then throws in another, "this is MY WEDDING," stomping her foot to emphasize who's wedding it is (and that evidently a child is being married off). "You had no right to have them switch seats."

The groom walks over and says, "what is going on?" in absolute dismay. The bride and I start explaining the situation, competing for who is loudest and right-est.

The groom ushers us fuming ladies into the hall where the bride tearfully cries with her finger in my face, "It's my day and you ruined it!"

The parents shuffle out to the hall to get in on the drama. The bride yells out my most horrible transgression and I turn to them with arms outstretched expecting to meet their eyes in agreement at the ridiculousness of this charade, but they are all giving me dirty looks.

I start to cry. I truly don't see what the big deal is. Off I run to the bathroom where my hair starts to fall out of its updo. Now this is bad. My hair cannot fall down.

Rushing through the door is the angry bride, screaming more obscenities at me, and interrupting my mini melt down. I meet her in the well-lit lounge area and unleash, "you are being ridiculous! If I have to hear 'it's my day or my wedding' one more I am going to vomit."

She sneers, gets in my face, and pushes me. I gasp, then I push her, and I see a bobby pin fly out of her hair. Her hair starts falling apart.

I stand there watching her fall apart in silence, not sure whether to be disappointed that my creation isn't holding up or to be ecstatic that my true revenge is playing out without my really having to plan it. Her mother flies in, the groom's mother saunters in followed by my sister ready for the show. The mother of the bride beckons in a hushed tone, "everyone can hear you, stop yelling, clean yourself up, and get back out there."

The bride kicks open the bathroom door with all the rage imaginable for a drunk, pissed off bride.

I wait a few minutes, regaining my fortitude to smile, then go outside with my sister. We sit in silence. Tears roll down my face as I try halfheartedly to blot them up.

I look at her and mumble, "it's just a meal."

My sister replies, "it's her day" and we both heartily laugh.

The groom walks up behind us, leans in close and whispers, "were you the one that farted at the alter?"

I look up at him. Through tears and I shrug my shoulders. Another bobby pin falls out and I hang my head.

He says, "Only you would have gas on my day."

The Gas Station Story

"Beauty comes from the inside and by 'the inside' I mean

the inside of the hair salon."

-Unknown

My mother, Bea, flings the doors to the salon open and parades through, moving with intention. She is a speed boat and the rest of us are dancing around in her wake as she heads to my chair.

"What's the rush?" I chide when I catch up. I look at her face and add, "What's with the bad mood?"

"I have a lot to tell you about my trip to Las Vegas with your dad and uncle I don't want you to rush me like you always do," she explained while straightening her clothing in the mirror.

I ignore her ruse and ask, "why did you change your appointment three times this week?"

"I am trying to get out of that house as much as possible. I didn't want to turn down any invitations that popped up. And a few popped up. I'm here now. Let's get started," my mother huffed with a dignified pain in her voice.

"What's going on at home?" I asked, opening the flood gates.

The story surges out of her refined demeanor, "You have no IDEA the HELL I have been living through since last weekend!"

Bring on the drama, I think.

I know my father is a pistol, but every week brings something else.

As my mom reaches for her bag and unabashedly produces a box bulging with pastries - cream cheese, chocolate and raspberry jam on top. Her sadness becomes apparent. Some cry, some mope, some shop, she eats sweets. She is protective of her suffering. She would never let my father see the evidence. He would relentlessly poke fun, so she smuggles them into her safe spaces and indulges in her sorrow.

I didn't have breakfast, so I grab the chocolate one.

We eat in silence, both preparing for the event ahead. After half the donut, I say, "let's get you washed."

The journey to the sinks is like a funeral procession. Her silence speaks volumes.

Isabella yells across the salon, "are those donuts!?" She simply looks at me and gives a single nod.

"Only one!" I yell back. I can tell she is tired. She should have so much to say about two of her four donuts disappearing. I wash her hair in silence.

We return to my chair and Isabella takes a seat next to us. Everyone finishes their donut in silence.

As the last morsels disappeared and fingers were licked clean, I asked, "how was Las Vegas? I know you won money. You always do," I mousse up my hands and get into the rhythm of my work. Today is only a blow-dry, so I can do it in 30 minutes. I gave her 45, though, because she sounded desperate on the phone.

Isabella leans in, we are waiting for a response. She takes a deep breath and sighs.

"I have been dying to tell you what happen on our way home from Vegas. I haven't told a soul because I am so embarrassed. And your father warned me if I told anyone, especially you kids, he would divorce me."

"Spill it," I say. We've heard that one so many times it's not even a threat anymore.

"This one's bad," she moaned. "He might. Or at least make my life a living hell!"

"Isn't it already!" I joked and Isabella and I laughed. She did not. Isabella and I exchange "oh crap," looks and quickly button it up.

66

My mom is looking at the floor and gathering her thoughts (or waiting for our full attention). She lifts her head and begins....

The blow dryer was on high at this point which normally is not an impediment to juicy storytelling around here. But today, her voice was low and strained. I switch off the blow dryer and say, "start over, I can't hear you with the dryer going."

She responds with a wave of her hand, "put it on low and then maybe you won't rush me. This is going to take a while." She begins again...

She sets the scene and barely gets us to Vegas before the hairdresser from the adjoining station approaches with her client.

She says, "shit, I don't want everyone to hear this."

We beckon and she starts again. I lean in, Isabella leans in, and the blow dryer leans in. She's dead serious. I never see her like this. Isabella and I lock eyes and know this is going to be good.

"You know when your father gets with his brother, it's like I don't even exist," she starts low and slow with all the suspense of a ghost story. "Well, the drive to Vegas was typical. Boring. No one talking to me, but your dad and Uncle Pete were chatting away about old times." She starts to loosen as her story unfolds. "I read my magazines. We had fun in Vegas. I didn't see them much. We met up for dinner every night and your father asked every night, 'Did you win anything?' I would always say no, but I was up every day." Now, she's getting into it. Her voice is low but the mom I know is in full form. "I won a little each day, but I wasn't going to tell him because he would want my money!"

"Yes, yes, we know," I said.

Isabella breaks in, "Got any to spare?" she pats her leg and said, "yes honey, I have some for you."

"Can we get back on to the story," I prodded.

"As usual, when we drive anywhere your uncle gets in the front seat and I am always in the back seat," her mom explains.

"Yes," I say, "I know."

"Well, we get to Kingman, Arizona and take a pit stop, get some gas, go to the bathroom. Your Dad pulls up to the gas pump. I begin to open my door and I accidentally hit your uncle in the ass with the car door. He jumps a little and I start to laugh and apologize, and he starts to laugh and farts at the same time. Then we both laugh again and I shuffle off to go the bathroom. I was running because I had to go number two."

I pipe in, "you mean diarrhea."

"Yes, yes," she waves her hand. "He always makes me so nervous when he drives. So, I barely make it to the bathroom. I thought I was going to shit my pants!"

We all start to laugh out loud. The hairdresser next to me turns around and interjects, "what are you laughing at? What did I miss?"

My mom snaps at her, "Shut up and turn around. This conversation is private!"

A smile spreads across my face. Now mom is back. Everyone knows my mother. Don't take it personally.

"Keep your voice down. I don't want anyone else to know what we are talking about. So, I was in the bathroom a while. My stomach was bad, and I know this is the last stop until we get to Phoenix, so I had to make sure it was all out," she said with her matter-of-fact flair.

"Then," she is really gesturing now, "I go outside, headed to where the car was and there was a different car parked at the pump. So, I looked on the side of the store. No car. No dad. No Pete. I start to walk all around the gas pumps and then run out to the street and there goes the car. YOUR FATHER IS HEADED EAST BOUND TO PHOENIX!" She yells out as soon as I turn off the blow dryer. Everyone in the salon looks over to us. I wave them off with a serious head shake so they all know to mind their own business. "All I saw was dust blowing down the road and a tumble weed blowing across the street." She extends her hand in the direction of the probably fictional tumbleweed, then draws it into a fist and pulls it in toward her heart as she continues, "I start yelling, calling his name and waving my hands, but he kept driving. I run down the street - and you know I don't run."

Isabella's mouth is hanging wide open and nothing coming out. I am just looking at her, my hands frozen in place.

"That son of a bitch left me at the gas station!" She pounded the words out with fists and stomps. The veins in her neck were visible and the corners of her mouth turned down as she pursed her lips shut.

Now my mouth is wide open, "he left you?"

"Yes!" she yells out loud again. Isabella still hasn't said a word. I take a deep breath, buying time to figure out how to respond when she holds up a finger, "Wait, I am not done with this story."

"There's more? Dear God," I say, exasperated.

"People are looking. They probably thought I was crazy or something. So, I just stand there outside in the street and realize I have no purse, no money, no cell phone,

NOTHING. So, I thought, he will realize I am NOT IN THE BACK SEAT in a few minutes and he will turn around. So, I am standing in the sun in the street, and 5 minutes, then 10 minutes go by, then 15 minutes and now I am PISSED!" She seethed as she relived the memory.

"By now my stomach is real upset so I go back in the store, hit the bathroom again and then go directly outside to see if he is back. No. He. Is. Not." Her face is quite red as she pauses for dramatic effect. "So, I then walk over to the clerk behind the counter and tell her what happened and ask to use her phone to call the police. And do you know what, she said I wasn't allowed to use the phone and said 'I am sure he will come back for you.'" She mocked the clerk's voice and then reenacted her own venomous response, "YOU DON'T KNOW MY HUSBAND. CALL THE POLICE! I have been here for 30 minutes already. If he knew I was gone he would have come back."

I am curling her hair in slow motion; every curl was beginning to be a masterpiece because I was so zoned in on the story.

She goes on, "Finally, she let me use the phone to call the police. I explained what happened and the officer asked if I am in any danger. He thought this was a domestic issue. I was a little saucy with him and said NO! He is just old and doesn't care about me so why would he look in the back seat to see if I was there. Will you please get him? So, I explained he was on his way back to Phoenix in a blue car."

I broke in, "A blue car? Don't you know the make and model of your car?"

"All I know is it is a Pontiac. And it's blue. I know, I know," She waves her hand, "I should know."

"I sit in that gas station for a total of two and half hours!"

"WHAT!" I jeered.

"Yes. No money, no nothing. That lady behind the counter never offered me a drink," She sniffed.

She continues in a perfunctory way, "The police catch up with him on highway I-40. They pull him over."

"They pull him over!?" Isabella and I say in unison.

She quips, "How else are they going to stop him? They had to pull him over. Let me finish my story. Stop interrupting me."

"Ok, ok, go on," we say.

"The police officer told me after they both get back to the gas station; he pulled him over with sirens and all. When the police officer walked up to the window Frank Sinatra was blaring from the radio. Could you see those two just singing away to Frank?" Isabella and I nod our heads. She goes on, "The police officer asked your dad to turn the music down, so he did. Then your father said 'why did you pull me over? I was going the speed limit.' 'Are you missing something?' Your father goes 'like what?' The police officer leans in the window and asked your uncle 'you missing anything?' Your uncle goes 'like what?' Your father goes 'is this a joke?' The police officer taps the back window and says, 'YOUR WIFE!' Your father jumps up and looks behind him and says, 'Where's Bea?' Your uncle repeats it, 'where's Bea?'" She shakes her head, "what asses."

Continuing on, "Your father yells out 'Where the hell is she?' The police officer says 'right where you left her.' Now your uncle filled me in on all this part. Your father said, 'I didn't leave her.' The police officer said 'yes you did, sir. She is waiting for you to pick her up back at the bathroom.' Then they turned around and had to drive back to Kingman and your uncle said every other word was 'F%$$ this' and 'F%$$ that' and how stupid I WAS!

"What, he was blaming you?" I asked, shocked.

"Oh, he blamed me all right! When he pulled up two and a half hours later, I was so pissed, I was ready for him! Your uncle came in and apologized, warning me that your father was so mad at me for not getting back into the car and that I embarrassed him with the police!"

My next client is in the waiting room. I put up a finger and pantomime 'a few more minutes' because I need to make sure the story is over. Oh, and it is not.

"I get in the car and your father is beet red. His face is like a lobster. I knew he was going to let me have it. Your father starts in 'What the hell were you doing?' 'What was I doing? I was going to the bathroom. Pete knew I was in the bathroom because I hit his sorry ass with the door! Plus, we all said we were going to the bathroom, that is WHY we stopped!' I was in no mood for his excuses. I said, 'why didn't you do a head count before you drove off?' Your father yells at the top of his lungs, 'next time I will. I will look in the back seat, then I will look in the trunk.' I yell out 'THE TRUNK?!' He yells back, 'yes, the trunk!'" A full-on Italian argument is being reenacted by my mom with hand gestures and different voices and it's all happening at full volume by now.

"Dear God, he is a piece of work," Isabella says in dismay. "Papa is losing it. Wait, did he ever say he was sorry?"

"No, we still are not talking. I leave each day because he is so nasty," She pulls a piece of candy out of her purse and slips it into her frown. "You can't tell anyone."

I gasp, "Are you kidding me?! I am going to tell my closest 100 friends! This is the best story yet!"

I spin the chair around to face my mother into the mirror. "He has to own this one. This is his fault. Period. Sorry it happened. But, your hair looks AWESOME."

Bea hits my arm and says, "See, if you don't rush, you will do my hair like a queen. Like I deserve."

I said, "Ok, you got me there. I will own that one. You deserve more time."

My mother truly looks sad. But, her hair really looks good.

There is a saying I heard form Garth Brooks, "In every blessing there is a curse, and in every curse there is a blessing." My Mom, more blessed than most.

When Life Dumps on You

"You can't always expect to always have a good hair day!"

-Unknown

After two full years of cutting hair, armed with the wisdom and fortitude that only a twenty-year-old has, I left the corporate gig to go out on my own. A small, quaint salon had an opening nearby that offered me the freedom to work for no one but me. The building was miniscule – three stations squeezed into an afterthought on an addition to an existing storefront. You had to know it was there and circle around a dank alley to access the place. An older gentleman owns it and uses it as haphazardly as his expectations for me. I jumped at the chance to make my own rules and hours. I spent much of the time alone.

Reclining in the salon chair with my feet propped up on the counter, tv on in the corner with something really steamy going on, smacking gum, magazine in my lap, and phone to my ear, I felt truly free. I was making my own way, without the help of parents, and I was spending my time in my own way, without the input of a boss micromanaging my time. I could sport my own look. I could work my ass off or goof off according to what I decide.

It was a Friday morning when I discovered the dark side of this freedom.

"Ding" goes the bell on the door and I look up from my book. I casually get to my feet and welcome the middle-aged man standing in the doorway.

"Can I get a haircut?" he asks without meeting my eyes.

"Sure!" I say with all the enthusiasm of a kid with business coming to find her, "I can do it right now!"

He nods without saying anything and takes a seat in the chair, still warm from my time spent there.

Hmm, a quiet one, I think to myself while brushing off the first inkling of uneasiness.

I am here for walk-ins. In fact, no one is scheduled to come in all morning. This thought starts to occur to me in a different way than it did in the previous few minutes. No one is coming here for hours.

I approach him and notice his hands clenched in his lap and his gaze down and slightly to the side. He's not taking in his image in the mirror and making judgements about the length or style of his hair the way most clients do. He's staring at the ground and doesn't look up when I arrive. I hesitate a moment before draping the cape over his body and snapping it at the back of his neck. He sits perfectly still. Surely, this is when he'll engage in the specifics of his haircut. Surely, he'll look me in the eyes and say, "just a little off the sides, please."

Nothing.

"So, have you been in before?" I manage in a desperate attempt at small talk.

"No."

I make the decision to spray his hair down instead of offering the customary shampoo and scalp massage. Without chit chat, he can be out the door in ten minutes. Just get this over with, I tell myself.

I go through the motions, spraying and combing through his hair. I start to sweat. I raise my hands with my professional tools and see them trembling ever so slightly. He hasn't glanced up, he hasn't spoken. How can the absence of these small, but normal things strike so much fear in me, I wonder. I start cutting. I am working fast– blazing through, then I notice a rhythmic movement under the cape. I hear a slight swishing of something moving back and forth under the sag of the polyester fabric. He's just nervous, I force myself to think. He's tapping his foot or patting his leg. Surely.

The only sure thing was that he'd been caught. He realizes his time here is finite and, since I'm not exactly a psychiatrist, I am not sure if this was his 'oh shit' part or 'oh yeah' part.

He drops his head and slouches lower in the chair. The movement and the swishing are getting faster and louder. I lurch away from him. A million thoughts race through my head before I scream. He knows I'm here alone. What if he hurts or rapes me? How do I get out of here? There are people outside – will they help me? I have scissors in my hand – can I defend myself?

Finally, I hold up the scissors between the two of us and I yell, "WHAT THE HELL ARE YOU DOING?"

He doesn't stop. He doesn't break his rhythm. He keeps right on beating off until, yes, he dumps his load right there on the cape.

I scream, loud this time, no audible words, just a blood curdling scream. I stagger away from the chair, still holding the scissors between the two of us.

The man jumps up and runs out of the salon. He disappears around the corner, leaving me stunned, shaking, heart pounding, and utterly alone. Grateful for the loneliness.

The beginning of unfortunate events working in salon…. Now to the big show.

You're Fired!

"When life does not allow you to change anything, get a

new haircut."

-Unknown

It turns out managing employees is the hardest part. It took the first two years of owning my salon to get the employees right. I was 29 years old when I opened on my own and had been cutting hair for eleven years. I was promoted to assistant manager at almost every place I had previously worked. I certainly had no formal business training. I learned on the job and I was pretty confident in my ability to pick the right people.

My salon has nine hair stations, four nail tech stations, a massage room, and a facial room. When I opened, I had two receptionists - day and evening shifts. I had all nine hair stations filled, all nail tech stations filled, and I had two massage therapists that split the room and they worked out the schedule and just paid me rent.

I do not like confrontation. I avoid arguing. I really was a people pleaser in those days. I placed everyone's happiness above my own.

This particular day, the salon was buzzing. Every hairdresser was there, they were moving through the place somehow managing not to collide, the phone was ringing off the hook, hair dryers were humming, scissors were snipping, brushes were clanging on trays, conversations and laughter punctuated the scene. And it would be the first day I fire someone.

No one ever teaches you the best way to let someone go. Is there really ever a good way? I don't think so. It's ugly, hurtful, embarrassing.

I am the first to admit I should not have done it in the middle of that bustling day. In the middle of that crowded place. With a client waiting. I just wanted it over with.

This particular massage therapist was not a good fit. No one liked her in the salon, her clients complained about her massages, she was always late, and she talked through massages which people hate – especially my mother, and my mother wasn't going to quit until I do something about it.

I scheduled an appointment to meet with my problem employee. I should have known squeezing her into a break in the middle of my day was a flawed idea, but I did it anyway.

She was running late. She asked the receptionist who answered her call if I could just talk to her over the phone.

"No, she has to come in," I relayed back to her through the intermediary. Because she has to take her stuff out of here, I finished in my head.

She strolls in two hours after I expected her. I was with a client. I asked her to wait in the massage room.

"I only have ten minutes," she snapped as she stomped back to the massage room and let the door slam behind her.

I had already explained to my client in a blur of nervous chatting what was about to happen.

"Go take care of it," she encouraged, obviously enjoying the dramatic energy of my mess.

That is another issue. I am in the habit of telling my clients everything that goes on behind the scenes. Stupid, but I do it. And they love it.

So, with a salon full of people, I confront the massage therapist.

I enter the massage room, note the diffused scent of lavender, and wonder how potent it's calming effects are. Nitrous Oxide might be more appropriate for this encounter. I keep my eyes glued to the floor until I've mustered enough courage to start. I had rehearsed my speech, debating being quick and curt or flowery and long winded to soften the blow. In this moment, I forgot my plan and went with:

"It's not working out. I have to let you go."

Well, let's just say it wasn't received well. She might not have been able to read a clock or give a massage, but she was a regular thesaurus for creative words meaning "bitch."

I took it.

"Can you take your personal items now?" I asked, suddenly very interested in the floor again. All I can think of is how they say not to look a wild animal in the eyes because they'll think you're challenging them to a fight. I hoped to subdue her.

She throws a diffuser across the room. She clears the cart with a sweep of her forearm. The crashing and banging and cussing are definitely audible outside.

I back toward the door and let myself out into the general area. Every single person is staring in silence. I return their stares with wide eyes and a helpless, shocked expression.

The massage therapist flies out of the door, shouting more obscenities. She explains to the whole room what a bad owner I am. She declares no one should work for me. She storms past me to the front door. Everyone swivels in their chairs to follow her boisterous promenade. As she reaches the front door, hand on the knob, she turns to look me squarely in the eyes and screams at the top of her lungs, "EAT ME!"

Then more. Over and over again she shouts, "EAT ME, EAT ME, EAT ME!"

Finally, she flings open the door and storms out, leaving us in deafening silence.

After an uncomfortably long pause, in which I am trying to grasp what exactly just happened, I hear, "that went well," mumbled by the receptionist. Her head is hung, and I can't see her face, but I notice her shoulders shaking in barely controlled laughter.

I can't help it. I start to laugh too. The tension flows out of me in fits of giggles and tears.

I turn to face the whole salon and I apologize to the dumbstruck faces. A few of my besties mouth "eat me" through smiles and I flip them off in return.

"Eat me?" I question as I return to my client. "What does that even mean?"

It was an ugly ending, but those usually bring about the biggest learning curves.

My next massage therapist was a blessing. She stayed with me until the very end. When there is darkness, there is always light on the other end.

Is Three a Crowd?

"The best hairdresser never stops learning."

-Unknown

I have 180 clients; few of them are couples. The ones I do have, rarely come in together.

I met the man first. He was referred by a friend and is an absolute joy. He loves to talk. He sparks up conversations with whoever is before and after him. He is pure entertainment. His carefree, jovial laugh warms the room and softens the stiffest of clients.

I cut his hair for about six months before his wife comes in. She is quiet, cold, uncomfortable, and closed off. She says she had a bad experience and just prefers to cut her own hair now.

After a few appointments, she starts to loosen up. She begins to share endearing stories and laughs with freedom, bringing an air of lighthearted joy.

After a couple more appointments, they get more and more comfortable with me. They start to share all the details of their personal life. Now, I'm no stranger to oversharing, but these details were remarkable.

I start to notice she is never wearing a bra. I shrug it off - how liberating that could be for some. She became noticeably more touchy with me. Hugs were different. Her whole body would press up against mine in a way that was foreign to most business embraces. She would grab my hand when I was talking and stroke my arm in a gentle and sensual display. She started to describe how she admires the curves of women's bodies…that women are so beautiful naked…how she loves to see women naked. Slowly, probably too slowly, it crossed my mind that maybe this woman is hitting on me. I thought, "Mia, get over yourself! She knows you are straight and she is married to a man."

She then asked me if I had ever gone to this particular bar "for swingers"?

I said "swingers, like a playground? Oh, as in swapping partners?" I tried to play my naïveté off as a joke but was definitely late to the adult conversation. "Oh, heavens no, not me," I laughed and almost literally clutched my pearls.

Lasagna recipes. She changes the subject fast.

A couple days later, her husband comes in for a haircut and is blandly chattering away about the weather or something, when he, as coolly as ever, sneaks in a, "hey, by the way, have you ever watched another couple have sex in person?" I swear I almost cut my finger off. My mind plays a track of records screeching, water spitting.

My face registers a look of shock plainly displayed in the mirror in front of us, but he goes on with the details about how he and his wife go to a bar and she finds a woman she likes and they take her home and he watches her with this woman and he beats off in a chair in the corner of the room while they do it.

"Oh?" I exhale, with my mouth agape. With my head spinning, I think of the most politically benign thing I can say, "You guys are living on the wild side. Good for you both!"

He goes on. I am a people pleaser, so I listen as he provides even more details. Now most people would have said, "Ok, I don't need to hear this" or "I'm uncomfortable" or "Too personal" or "STOP," but no, I keep listening and smiling.

He then goes on, plain as day, about the rules. "After the women are done, I jump in the mix. I'm not allowed to screw the new girls, only my wife. And the third wheel can do whatever she wants, but no sex with me."

Again, I mumble a noncommittal and nonjudgmental statement, but I'm running low on responses, "Free spirits you guys are! Good for you both!" Followed by awkward, nervous giggles.

He continues, because of course he does. "We really enjoy going to swingers' clubs and my wife really likes women and I am open to that exchange."

I couldn't stop myself, "will you let her do another man?"

"Oh no," he said with a jolt, like this was the weird part of the conversation, "that is off limits, just women."

"Well, you have to be strong in your marriage to share one another," I optimistically tried.

He goes on. Every weekend they do this. They go to bar or the swingers club and pick someone up. They have done this for years.

I asked "how many years?"

He said "14 years."

I thought I would shit my pants. "What? Your whole marriage?"

"She told me on our very first date that she liked women, too. And I said I loved that. And that is why we've been married so long. We've both had been married a few other times and I knew this one will work because it sure stays spicey!"

Once again, "Good for you both!"

Then there was silence for a few minutes. To tell you the truth, I knew it was coming.

He said, "Mia, I have to ask you something. My wife was too shy to ask and she didn't want to embarrasses herself if you didn't say what she wanted to hear."

Oh God, here it comes.

"We would love for you to be our threesome."

I stopped cutting his hair and said "What? Me? Oh no, not me. I have never. Isn't three crowed in one bed?" I nervously fished for excuses, then started to laugh, trying to shut the conversation down.

He was not dissuaded by subtle attempts at not fainting. He goes on about how his wife is attracted to me and she wanted to ask me when she was here the last time but she chickened out.

I said, "well, I am honored, but I have to say no. I see enough of women's conch's doing bikini waxes and I can say unequivocally, I am not attracted to that. Really, they smell…most of them smell." Who am I? Am I saying that out loud to a client?

He goes on to say that's what he loves about a woman, their scent.

"You call it scent!?" I ask. Oh, is this really happening? My efforts to shut this down are getting me in deeper.

"Thank you for thinking of me, but I am out," I told him.

He said, "Think about it. You answered too quickly."

"Really no time needed…Three is a crowd for me."

Yoga as Therapy

"A good stylist is cheaper than a good therapist."

-Joan Crawford

I was 15 years into doing hair when I discovered yoga. My entrée was nothing really, a client who did not practice it, mentioned she'd heard good things. Looking back, it's scary how casually a life changing discovery can enter your life.

I was wearing flats. That's all, really, that sparked my client's life changing topic of chit chat. She notices right away that I'm not in my usual high fashion, dress-for-success ensemble. I was told an owner of a salon should stand out of the crowd, so, I brought style every day - pointy, red, high heels and more flash the higher up you look.

This morning, though, my lower back was killing me before my feet left the bed. When they touched the ground and the weight of my body pressed them flat to the floor, I had to squeal from the ache. I waddled, hunched over, groaning with each shift and step. I rationalized taking it easy which meant cotton and flats (and extra lipstick).

"What do you have going on after work, why are you dressed like that?" My longtime client asked.

"I hurt all over," I confessed. "I worked twelve hours yesterday, then I went running six miles with my girlfriend and I think my body is barking back. I couldn't do ten hours in heels today."

"I've heard yoga helps." She didn't know she lit the first spark.

Yoga was not popular at that time. There was only one studio in all of Phoenix. And I'll be damned if there wasn't a coupon for it in the mail that day.

The following week with two random signs and my curiosity piqued, I tried it out. I had no idea what I was getting into and I surely wasn't dressed properly. I wore basketball shorts and a baseball hat (don't ask me why).

A middle-aged, very friendly man greeted me from the front desk with a gentle smile and odd slowness about him. I was immediately struck by his welcoming contentment. He asked with a knowing smile if I had ever tried yoga. I said no, but I am exploring ways to help with my aching body. We have a short conversation in which I tell him what I do for a living and he genuinely laughs despite, or because of his baldness. I sign up for the week.

There is a wall separating the entrance from the studio. The room is miniscule and in its emptiness, does not seem capable of curing my pain. I look around skeptically before I spot the bathroom in the corner. I am so nervous; I dart in and relieve my tension. I exit into a room full of chatting and laughing yogis when the nice man from the front motions toward me (and the bathroom) and introduces me as the new girl. I sheepishly wave, drop my head, and wish to disappear into the back, left corner of the room. I find my mat there, and we begin.

I took dance my entire life so I thought I'd be prepared. Dear God and we are off - up and down and up and down and up and down. Ten minutes in and I am exhausted. The nice man from the front desk and bathroom introduction was seeming not so nice now. He moved fast, I barely kept up. This went on and on, I thought I was in a time warp. Then the moves change - same but different, up and down and up and down. The baseball hat was proving to be a very poor choice at this time, but *NO WAY* am I going to take it off and reveal my hat hair to these oblivious yogis. I'm truly dying at this point. Sweat is dripping from everywhere. I am getting mad, then I am getting sad, and then I get excited when I can successfully perform one of the moves. Oh wait, then I am mad again, and sad again. I am talking to myself the entire time, mumbling inspiration and curse words. I glance around the room at these beautiful, fluid movements executed with grace and strength and then I get competitive. I thought this yoga was calming, but now I'm sad, mad, embarrassed, and confused. My eye caught the door and I consider leaving, but pride keeps me on that mat until the end.

Finally, I am instructed to stretch – just slow down and hold a pose and relax and listen to the music. It is lovely, I don't understand a word but I'm in such a dreamlike state. Maybe it is my exhaustion, maybe it is the Sanskrit, but I am floating. The teacher is talking but I am not really taking it in. I am engrossed in bliss. It's like I'm at the beach and waves of serotonin are lapping over me.

But then, again I feel sad. It's like the tears well up in my eyes before I even feel the squeezing of my heart. I tell myself 'don't you cry" not here. What is happening? Then I hear him say "take a deep breath" and I did, but it gets stuck in my throat. "Slowly let it go. Slow the breath down," he says, so I do. It glides out smoother this time and I think I'm back in control. The instructor walks over and puts a hand on my back and says it again. He surely knows I am struggling.

Then he says it's over. "Go to your back and go in Savasana." I look around as everyone flops onto their back and lays there like sweaty starfish.

While lying there, tears immediately come to my eyes. I graciously have a towel over my eyes thank God he gives those out. The tears are just streaming from my eyes and I can't stop them. All can think is, I came here to help my feet and I don't get why I am crying. So, I cry.

It was the best 5 minutes I had in a long time. Lying still with no one bugging me, my feet didn't hurt, my back felt great, the tears just relieved the pressure I didn't know I could relieve.

I walk out last. "How was it?" he asked.

"Challenging, but I liked it. My whole body hurt before and I feel really good now," I offered, completely glossing over the emotional release I just uncorked in a crowded, sweaty room.

He lowered his eyes, smiled, and said, "yes, most people come for the physical but it's an emotional practice as well."

Be cool, I steadied myself, "Well, I could agree," I replied in an overly chipper coverup.

"A good cry always helps release the yuck we don't need."

My eyes get wide open and I say nothing except *shit* to myself.

"I hope to see you again. Yoga is great therapy for whatever you need to release."

Alright, it's out there in the open and I'm mortified, but also extremely grateful. "Yes, you will see me again and thank you," I mumble.

That was the beginning of some very cheap therapy for me and I never stopped going.

Yoga saved me from me. I went for the physical but found, very quickly, that it offers so much more. Yes, my back and feet never hurt again and my physique didn't suffer, but all that paled in comparison to the changes going on inside my head and heart.

Yoga teaches me that all those negative thoughts hurt my spirit and my soul, and everything that I EVER held onto emotionally wants to be released, but I never let it go. I grip, I hold tight and it does nothing but hurt me in the end.

There is a saying, *Let go or be dragged.*

I am a changed person to this day, thanks to yoga. It changed me, helped me, released me from the traumas, sadness and anger I had within. It has truly saved me, and continues to save me anew every day.

Yogash Citta Vritti Nirodha. Yoga is the cessation of the modifications, or fluctuations, of the mind. Many days I thought I would lose my mind but not today. Today I begin again.

The Pop In

"I play with scissors for the shear fun of it."

-*Anonymous*

The "busy-ness" of my business is notable. People are constantly coming and going and shouting their hellos and goodbyes and hugging old friends and gushing over new looks. The energy is magic, really. But, it is a controlled magic, a scheduled magic. Everyone has their time slot and I know to the minute how long Ms. O'Connor's story is going to take. Without fail, though, two people would "pop in" just to say hi, grab some coffee, pull up a chair, and catch up.

My background or heritage is 75% Italian and 25% Czechoslovakian. That little bit of Czech gave me the 5'9 height and the green eyes. So that is a blessing. My father's mother was from Czechoslovakia (thank God) so my father was half Italian and Czech and my mother was full bred Italian. All three of my Italian grandparents were from Sicily, Italy.

So that heritage is in me. I love being Italian - the food and the traditions we have are bigger than life, so when anyone figures out I am Italian and they are Italian it's over, we are family instantly. Bennie, a regular, embodies this jovial camaraderie in the form of his perpetual "pop in".

He knew my schedule; he knew when my daughter or sister would be working the front desk. It was like he knew when I was having a bad day, or just all around crazy day. He would just pop in.

When I see his face my heart smiles. I love this man with my whole being. My mother loves him, my kids love him, my clients love him, and the employees love him.

He is from Brooklyn, New York and full blood Italian. He is a big jolly man. You can smell his cologne as soon as he walks in the room. He is married with no kids. He was a grade school counselor, and he was a singer for his side job. Sometimes he would walk in singing Frank Sinatra! But most of the time, he would walk in and yell out, "Hello, beautiful women!" Everyone knows Bennie and everyone loves him. If he had never seen you before, he would introduce himself to you. He was that guy. The friendliest man I knew, and the nicest.

Bennie wouldn't pop in every week, but when he did, he made everyone's day. He lived right by the salon - within five minutes - so on his way home or on the way to the store he would stop by with a smile and a story.

Every story I told about him and every time he crossed my mind, he serendipitously popped in. "I knew you were thinking of me, that's why I came by," he'd wink. Now Bennie didn't come for the coffee, he came by to get a hug, grab a piece a candy or two at the front desk and fill us in on his singing gigs. He once gave me a cassette tape of his singing and wanted my opinion - he could sing. Sometimes he would sing to me in the chair.... It was lovely.

Now the other "pop in" was my Dad. When I told him I wanted to open up a hair salon, he told me I was crazy. He told me I had no business opening up a business. He also told me he would not help me with anything. It was all me. He made it very clear that he wanted nothing to do with this salon, yet there he sat, every week.

It took ten years of me cutting hair before he finally let me cut his in the salon. I am pretty sure he switched over to me because it was free (and there were always pretty women in the salon).

Now my Dad came like clockwork to get his hair cut. He would call the front desk so he could talk to my daughter, or he would just pop in and see if I was free. Most of the time he knew I was busy, but it gave him an excuse to come back a second time.

He would yell out every visit, "how old is the coffee?" Typically, we would make a fresh pot for himself and then he would pull up a chair at the front desk and talk to all the people coming and going. He would walk over to my station and joke with my client as only dads can do, "is she doing a good job?" They would always say yes and tell him how much they love me and he would just smile and take it all in.

The hair salon is a great place for any man to hang out. My dad loved it. He would never admit to it, but he smiled the whole time he was in the salon and I knew deep down he liked the place. Everyone knew him and he liked that. He was kind of a big deal in the salon and he liked that.

The Pole & Roof Top living

"Good hair does not stay home on Friday."

-Hidden Crown

"Shhh… What is that sound?"

Our Friday night pizza dinner tradition was interrupted by the first sounds of outdoor things clattering and raindrops whizzing from the sky. It was pretty typical in the middle of the summer to have a dry monsoon blow through, but if we got rain that was a miracle. Well, the miracle was happening, and we halted everything to rush outside and dance in the warm, wet evening.

When the doorbell rang there was our pizza delivery boy, (yes, he was boy), drenched like a pitiful dog. No umbrella, no jacket, just one large cheese and one large pineapple and Canadian bacon pizzas. The boxes were soaked.

I asked, "no umbrella?" he shook his head. "It's raining pretty bad tonight. You been busy?" He shrugged his shoulders.

I handed him his money and a five dollar tip. He looked at it, then looked me right in the eye and stood there with his hand held out.

"I am divorced and have three kids, sorry man," I said as I closed the door.

It rained all night. It wasn't just a monsoon it was a real storm and a welcomed one. It hadn't rained in ages.

Saturdays are busy in the salon. I have "all hands on deck," so they say, so I try to get there early to get things set up. I pull up to the salon and see palm tree branches littering the parking lot and leaves and tumbleweeds stuck to the building.

I look around in dismay, but the real shock hits me when I walk inside. The salon has a waterfall right through the middle of it. The roof caved in, leaving a gaping, dripping view of the blue sky outside.

I call the rental company and get to cleaning up the mess before clients begin to arrive. The maintenance guy shows up an hour later and he says he needs to get on the roof to check it out. He was back down before I could find a broom and said, "ma'am, I'm going to need to talk to you." He began with, "well, it seems we have two problems."

I nodded, "just tell me." There's a hole in the ceiling, what could top that?

"I think there are people living on your roof," he smirked, trying to maintain a professional demeanor.

My mouth opened wide and before I get a word out and he continues, "I think they are homeless."

I said, "what?" then gave him a puzzled look.

He says "I know for sure I am going to have to put a pole in the middle of your salon so the roof doesn't cave in completely because they have a couch, a chair and personal belongings up on the roof and the whole roof is caving in and with this much damage and the furniture that is up there, it could get ugly."

He leaves and comes back two hours later with a pole - a silver steel pole to put right in the middle of the salon, from floor to ceiling. He continued to tell me that he couldn't work on the roof for a month because he had other jobs to do first and this pole would be fine until then.

"Well, that's classy," I think. "Girls, we're signing up for pole dancing classes!"

If we have a pole in the middle of the salon, let's figure out what to do with it.

A girlfriend and I sign up for a four-week session. I figure embracing it (with my thighs) was the only option. We go once a week for two hours and we learn how hard it is to pole dance. I couldn't even hold myself up the first week. What started as a silly joke, became a character-building endeavor. I was determined. Every week I improved. I was a little embarrassed, I'll admit. I didn't plan on taking it seriously, but it was that or quit. And I was not going to fail at pole dancing when I had to look at one all day, every day. I was wearing high heels and skin-tight clothes and owning the whole scene. For all of my effort to be graceful and sexy, I know I looked like a slug making a slow, sad dissent down the pole.

The last night of the session, we had a mini show and could invite a small audience. I was going to whip this slug up on the pole, swing my feet above my head, hug the pole with my legs, go upside down, then slide down and then flip myself standing upright. It was all very spectacular in my head.

Showtime came, and I did it. I grab that pole, flip my feet over my head in a dramatic display of strength and grace. Then I hear a pop and felt the burn in my left arm. Despite the pain, I am upside down, legs are wrapping around the pole, suspending me in the air like a desirable trapeze artist. I AM POLE DANCING. I feel the glory of the stage and the freedom of the dance, and when my pride has all but burst into confetti - I fall to the floor - no big graceful ending - just me on my head on the floor and only one arm strong enough to pick myself up.

Everyone is clapping.

I bow as I say, "My career of pole dancer is over. I just tore my triceps."

The instructor says, "Oh that happens a lot." As I lay on the floor holding my tricep, I shouted out, "By the way, I have a roof top for rent if anyone is interested"

Why Me?

"When you look in the mirror & think, did I really look like

that all day?"

-Unknown

I put a lot of thought into my wardrobe. I need to be comfortable and professional. Shoes I can stand in for ten hours aren't always the hottest thing on the shelf, but I manage. Today, I'm feeling a bit free, like a 60's flower child. So, I grab my floor length, multi-colored skirt and pair it with a funky vest (yes, a vest) and a plain t-shirt. The best part is my Birkenstock shoes. They scream peace and patchouli. I punctuate the ensemble with a mala bead necklace and funky bracelets. I am feeling the ethos of the decade of love. I flash my two peace fingers at my reflection in the mirror and start my day.

Saturdays are a buzzing blur at the salon. We don't even sit down to eat. The receptionist orders in and we just grab a mouthful when we can and get on with the next client.

Isabella walks in with three bags of food releasing the most mouth-watering aroma. Chinese stir fry beacons me to take a break. By a small miracle I had a gap in clients and practically float to the back room like a cartoon character sniffing a ribbon of enticing scent.

I shovel in most of my lunch like a ravenous animal. It was cashew chicken with fried rice and a few egg rolls...I love that! As I was eating, I was saying to myself "Oh, this is so good. Oh, this is so, so good". No sooner do I move on to the egg rolls, then one of the girls pops her head in and announces my next client is waiting. I chew, wipe my face, brush the rice off my front and rush to my station.

I'm already planning my return to my remaining lunch when I greet him. As usual, hugs are exchanged, small talk begins and then we head to the shampoo bowls. As I am shampooing, I feel a sharp pain in my side and then a hot flash. I pause. My client, oblivious to my internal situation, chats on. Isabella exits the breakroom and looks straight at me. The look of worry on her face alerts me to the look of worry on mine.

I feel another sharp pain on my side. I try to maintain a semblance of professionalism as I push the client up from the chair. I motion him toward the station as I take stock of my situation. Isabella approaches and I whisper, "I think my stomach didn't like the food."

Isabella mouths, "SURGES!"

I frantically whisper, "shhhhh."

My client turned around and we smile our most cheerful everything-is-just -fine-grins.

As I begin to comb his hair, another surge. I maintain my smile while almost folding in half. He talks about who-knows-what while my mind is spinning with thoughts of, "Oh god I am going to fart, oh god I hope he can't hear my stomach, oh god I hope it is not what I think it is......"

He pauses and says, "Boy, your stomach is making loud noises. Do you need to eat lunch?"

"Yes," I blurted, as explaining that my belly was quite full of lunch and loudly expressing its discontent and I think I am going to SHIT my pants in a minute, would have been fairly awkward.

I start cutting faster as I notice the sweat bubble up on my upper lip. Now I am squeezing my butt cheeks with the desperation of a woman clinging to her last shred of self-respect.

I finish his haircut and think I'm in the clear. I rush his hug goodbye and yell at Isabella to take care of him. I muster every ounce of conviction to hold it in, send up a little prayer, and hobble toward the bathroom, not even trying to look cool anymore. I raise my eyes to zero in on my goal only to register the door is closed and the only bathroom is occupied.

DEAR GOD, PLEASE LET THAT PERSON COME OUT RIGHT NOW.

My free love hippie skirt and tiny thong were starting to feel like catastrophic mistakes. The idyllic carefree spirit of the day had brought me to a painful shuffle across the lobby singing Bob Dylan's (slightly altered) refrain, "The answer my friend, is blowin' out my end. The answer is blowin' out my end." Then it happened. Step. Surge. Squirt. It went drip, drip, drip down my leg, then onto my shoe. Oh shit. Literally. Then the door swung opened and out ambled an unsuspecting guest as I stood in the throes of physical and social ruin. I smiled a very calm, regular hello to the client, then bolted in behind her. I locked the door, floundered to the toilet, and cramped and cleared it all out. After a few minutes of my body being ravaged from the inside, I calm and take stock of my clothing situation. There it was on my shoes, on my legs, on the inside of my skirt.

I buried my head in my hands, began to cry, and tried to come up with a plan to finish my day.

There is a knock at the door. I sit bolt upright. Isabella yell-whispered through the crack, "are you ok?"

I unlock the door, frantically usher her in, and pitifully moan "look at me." I had my thong in my hand, shoes were off in the sink, and my skirt is hang drying over the towel rack.

"Nice vest," she says kindly.

Isabella races home, picks up a change of clothes, and is back before I can say Pepto-Bismol.

Meanwhile, I slip on my wet skirt, ditching the panties and shoes. I douse myself in lavender oil and get on with the day. Work ethic is one thing, but cutting hair barefoot and panty-free is quite another. When Isabella gets back, I whisper to cancel my day. I just want to go home.

Word has gotten around by this point. So, as I grab my stuff to head home, everyone starts to clap and heckle. I throw up my hands and shout, "WHY ME!" on my way out the door…

Private Detective

"...and then the humidity said today I'll make you look like

the Lion King."

-Unknown

I remember the day she walked in. She was young, smiling, cute, and fresh. Of course, I hired her for the receptionist position. I usually kept family up there, but I couldn't pass this lovely kid up.

She caught on quickly, she arrived on time, she dressed trendy, and she was so polite. Everyone liked her breezy, youthful flair in the salon. She made herself useful and joined in on the conversation. Really, a super cute kid.

Within a few weeks, the register started counting short at the end of the night - not by much, but five dollars here and then ten dollars there. I changed policy and made the receptionist start to count the money at the end of each shift to see where the mistakes were taking place. Then it stopped.

Days later, my nail technician came to me and said, quite sheepishly, "I think someone is taking money out of my nail station."

"You're sure?" I asked, with animosity building.

"Yes! I know how much money I make all day long and how much I bring in for change and I keep coming up short." She obviously hated to bring this to me.

"I'll keep an eye on your station," I promised, while devising a plan.

She said, "you better keep track of your money too."

It pained me to think that someone would steal from me, their boss, their employer, but - lo and behold - the next day I notice a $20 bill missing out of my money bag.

The next day another hairdresser said she was missing money out of her bag.

I couldn't believe it. Of course, the small group privy to the crime spree started speculating. We assumed, for obvious reasons, it has to be the new girl. Now we start devising a plan to catch her.

I tell one of my trusted clients about the issue and she mentions a detective store about ten miles away that has this powder you can put on things you're worried about going missing. If someone touches the powder, then gets her hands wet, it will turn them bright purple and does not wash off, then we will know it is her. Real detective shit. The very next day, I giddily pick up the small little canister and set the plan in motion.

I put fake money, painted in the clear powder in the front desk cash drawer. I load it with $100 dollar bills so it's very tempting to take. The nail tech stuffs her bag with booby-trapped cash as well.

That very night my nail tech/sidekick finds money missing. We initiate step two to get the perpetrator's hands wet. I casually ask her to wash the bowls in the back room sink for us because we are all running behind. She says she will. Everyone in the salon knows what is going down. We all wait.

Not surprisingly, we hear screaming coming from the back room. We rush in to find glowing purple hands and forearms waving around. The thief has no idea why her hands are purple and has no idea that she's been caught. But the rest of us are high fiving like a winning team.

"Sit down and don't move," I hiss. I finish up my client in an adrenaline laced rage. Then I call her parents and give them a short, non-comital explanation for needing to come to the salon.

I am greeted back at the break room with scared sobs. The fear and embarrassment I know she's feeling convinces me to take a deep breath and sit next to her. I say as calmly and serenely as possible, "we know you are the one stealing from all of us." I smile as I think about how much I want to pinch her and shout, "you little brat, what the f@#! were you thinking?!?" But I maintain my cool and just look her in the eye and asked, "why?"

She has the audacity to deny it, stammering, "I don't know what you're talking about."

"You have purple all over your hands," I point out.

"I must have touched something" she tries again.

I said, "you touched something all right, our money!"

She keeps repeating her innocence and I keep my accusation, over and over again to crack her like a detective would. I get a bit crazy.

Her parents finally show up. I explain how we have been having money missing, started with the register then, how I know it is her.

"Her hands are purple," I shout, then storm over to my station and pull out the detective powder. I explain my whole plan and how she is now caught 'purple handed'.

Her parents speechless, the young girl dumbfounded and me prouder than a peacock in the rain. Plus, purple just became my new favorite color.

Say Hello to my Little Friend

"Never, never, never give up on your hair."

-Unknown

What is it about a salon that brings out the crazies? Maybe it's me; maybe I invite them into my life. I invite some great ones too, don't get me wrong, but I have to think I get more than my share of the weirdos.

There must have been a full moon. I track it now, but back then I just noticed afterward that everything seemed off. The receptionist was late, the coffee pot leaked, the clients were grouchy. There was just a bad energy all around.

We are located in a normal retail store front with windows all the way across the salon covered by vertical blinds. Remember those? I hate them but they are cheap and they block out the Arizona heat. This particular night we didn't close them so everyone from the outside could see the illuminated interior, but we couldn't see out into the dark.

The receptionist seated up front noticed a man walking by that caught her attention. She approached me, saying "I may be crazy, but I have a bad feeling. He was wearing a coat and it's a hundred degrees out there."

I flippantly suggested to lock the door and went back to work on my last client for the night, not giving it too much thought.

As we finish, I escort the client to the front, hug and wish her goodnight. The receptionist and I stand in the entrance, doors flung open, hands waiving, sighs of a completed day at last.

There is the coat man standing right in front of the window, coat wide open. Under the inappropriate jacket is an even more inappropriate surprise. He is wearing only a woman's underwire bra and sneakers. His eyes are locked on mine and a strange look of pleasure and exertion punctuated his gaze as he starts going to town on his Johnson, yes, his willie, yes, his pecker. He was beating off as he watched us in the well-lit interior. The receptionist and I took a moment to process what we were seeing, then started to scream…AHHHH AHHHHH! I lunge for my phone, as I yell "call the police, call the police". Then I change my instructions to "lock the door, lock the door!" I can feel my heartbeat in my throat. My hands are trembling so much I can hardly dial the phone.

When he sees us making calls, he whips his coat closed and runs off into the night. I am shouting every cuss word I know and thanking the receptionist for locking the door and we grab each other and tremble together in a fearful embrace. I wanted to cry but I look at her and say let's get the F$@! out of here!

From that day forward, mace in the drawer and camera ready. Pictures might come in handy one day.

Opinions

"Sorry, I can't hear you over the volume of my hair."

-Unknown

A cancelation in my day becomes a blessing of "me time" on the yoga mat. Thursday mornings are typically quiet in the salon. To add to the nirvana, the night before I had a color and haircut cancel, so I don't have to go in the salon until 1:00 pm today. I take the whole morning to unwind in the yoga studio. Peaceful meditation transitions into an invigorating vinyasa class. Then, I stop for a smoothie on the way home. Purposeful self-care never felt so good. I take my time getting ready and head into the salon.

My 1:00 pm is a standing client. She comes in every 4 weeks without fail. Never cancels. Her hair is her everything. As I wait behind the chair looking at my phone, she approaches and jauntily says, "good afternoon."

I look up with a, "hello Lydia, how is it going?" greeting. She is a very polite woman, very proper and religious. She is always dressed in impeccably fitting clothes, a complementing belt with pristine matching ked sneakers. Her sleek purse is always on her shoulder and she walks with grace.

I follow up with, "the usual?" She replies, "Yes." I have done her hair for years and the details and conversation have been the same for ages. The color is 7N and a bob cut. Her life is her church. She only associates with church people and our conversations are always about the bible, God, and the Holy Ghost. Because she is very well mannered, she will very briefly ask about my kids and my parents. Then the conversation always settles onto her bible study group and what they discuss the week prior.

I am a good listener. I listen and nod a lot and make short responses like "Oh", "really", "nice", and so on. She subtly but still obviously does not like me squeezing anyone in while she waits with color on her hair, but sometimes that had to happen. This particular day, I squeeze an additional haircut in while she is sitting for the 40 minutes. I apologize and over explain to her I had cancellations this morning and in order to make up for the lost revenue, accepted a call this morning for the haircut.

She nodded politely and I handed her a few magazines and said, "you have 40 minutes. I will set a timer."

The interjected client is a single schoolteacher with the summers off so. She needed to be squeezed in today to prepare for a last-minute trip out of town. She is a different sort than Lydia and I became keenly aware of my dual identities as Lydia listens in to our conversation.

We hug as she walks in and we head to the shampoo bowls, chatting up a storm. I ask her how her summer is going and where she is headed off to. We get like two school girls when we get together. Lydia is sitting in the station next to mine and can hear our whole conversation.

"How is yoga going?", the new client casually asks.

And just like that, Lydia's head pops up from the magazine with all the alertness of a wild animal in stalking mode. She slaps her reading material down on her lap and stares right at me with squinted eyes of intense disapproval. My other client didn't notice and keeps on jovially asking about classes and mats and music and poses. I know exactly what Lydia was thinking. I have heard it before. "Yoga is the devil's work." I try to change the subject because she can hear everything, and I can practically feel her anger blistering into me.

But, oh no, my client isn't hearing of it. "Tell me everything!" she clamors on.

"I would rather hear about where you are going and how the dating life is… Any good prospects?" My client looks puzzled and as soon as Lydia looks the other way, I hit my client on the shoulder and give her the stink eye, motioning toward Lydia. A bit puzzled, she glances over at Lydia and now Lydia is giving her the stink eye. I secretively smacked her again with the comb on her opposite shoulder and I think she finally gets it… No talking about yoga. Very discreetly my client nods her head and begins talking about her trip and how she is going to visit her sister in California.

I finish the cut, we walk up to the front desk, and she whispers, "what the hell was that?"

I explain that Lydia is a very religious lady and I don't tell her about my private life unless I want a speech about how bad yoga is.

"Dear God," she replies. "I guess you have to eliminate some conversations to make peace."

Yes, Yes I do. It makes working conditions easier.

Back in front of Lydia, I am a naughty child, waiting to get a reprimanding. "Let's go back and shampoo you," I say, just waiting for it. She gets up stiffly and says nothing.

I can feel the tension in the air. She is gripping the magazines, her jaw is clenched, I finish her wash, dry her hair, and we walk back to my station. I grab a comb and scissors and begin cutting her hair. That's when the lecture began.

"Why do you do yoga? I thought you're a Christian," Lydia scolds.

"I started it because my whole body hurt from cutting hair and yoga makes me feel better," I say, calmly and mostly hiding the defensiveness.

She yelps out, "It's the devils' work!"

"I don't think it is," I reply, guarded, but casual.

"Yes, it's the devil! You are worshiping to Buddhas!" she says with a tone.

"No, we are not. It's just physical movement," I say very shyly.

She yells out for all to hear, "I have to pray for your soul. I am going to ask the holy ghost to help me save you!"

"No, no, really it is not like that...." I start, but am interrupted by a spinning chair as she whips around to face me, puts her hands on my head, and starts praying. I kind of jump back and she leans in. Her hand is on my forehead.

"I am trying to cut your hair," I point out.

She says nothing she just keeps praying out loud, saying stuff like "heal her dark side, remove the darkness, cleanse her soul, she believes in you, heal her Jesus, heal her....," over and over again.

While her hand is on my forehead, I begin to do a yogic breathing technique. I start to breath from the belly. I repeat internally, "I am breathing in and breathing out."

She cries out, "yes, breathe deeply get it out!"

I say to myself, "I love yoga, I love yoga, I am breathing in and I am breathing out." Meanwhile the praying is going on out loud. This went on for a very awkward ten minutes.

Finally, she turns around to the front of my station. Her eyes are still closed, and she holds her hands in the air and begins to make sounds like she is talking in a different language. I stop cutting her hair and watch, a bit confused. She opens her eyes and beckons me on. So, I do my best to not raise my eyebrows too much, and continue cutting her hair, and she resumes her weird language. Is this talking in tongues? She has told me about that she does this with people. And now I'm one of those people. I will take the prayer. Who doesn't need prayers?

When I finish her up, she stops praying. She looks me straight in the eyes and says, "You can't do yoga anymore. I removed the devil from your heart and you are good now."

I tell her, "thank you for that clearing. I am sure I needed it."

She stands up and gives me a huge hug and says, "I will be back tomorrow to do some more tongues on your space and you."

I told her "really, I think you did a great job. I feel good. I think I'm all cleared out."

She says as she holds my hand, "May God bless you each day."

I say, "thank you and you too."

She pays me and she says goodbye. I wave and say goodbye and under my breath I add "Namaste."

She turns her head back and says, "did you say something?"

"Nope." Big innocent dear eyes complement the lie.

She smiles and walks out.

That very day I realized opinions are like assholes - everyone has one.

Right Behind Your Back

"Hair doesn't make the woman, but good hair definitely

helps."

-Unknown

For all I know, it is going to be another enchanting day at the salon. I love my work, my community, my family, my haven. I love the hum of the dryers, the conversations punctuated with laughter. I love the smiles and the smells. This particular Friday is busy. All nine of the hairdressers, all three of the nail techs, and the massage therapist were in and doing their things. The whole family is together and I feel the pride of a matriarch at Thanksgiving. But, Friday is typically my half day. I go in for one of my favorite clients, Lola and also for my mother, Bea, then I devote the second half of the day to me.

There is no guilt involved in my guilty pleasure. I meet my dear friend and we shop, drink, unload, listen, laugh, and dream. We have kept this holy event going for years and it fuels me.

This particular Friday, I was knocking down challenges and rising to occasions as I squeezed my father in after my mother, a client who dragged her daughter in for a quick bang trim, an employee who just wanted me to apply color to her hair then she will go home and rinse it. All are innocent enough, but are starting to engorge my half day.

I am standing at my station waiting for my next client when I notice a new face. There are no clients that aren't friends or family. I practically live at the salon. I pride myself in knowing everyone who comes through my home.

But this lady is walking around the waiting room, pacing. I interpret her nervousness as a big change she might be making in her looks. We deal in divorce recovery, empty nest embracement, new career jitters, even coming to terms with death on a regular basis. Women wear their battles and victories outwardly for all the world to see.

Then my client's entrance sweeps all of my attention to her and her daughter and my schedule. It was 11:00 am and I have one hour until I am home free.

But, the receptionist reminds me that my bookkeeper is coming in to drop off the monthly paper work and I needed to leave a check. And that is where the magic of the day shifts into chaos.

I wrap up with my clients, kiss their cheeks, send them on their ways, bound to the break room to write that check and notice two checks are missing. Hmm, I puzzled as I try to remember what I would have written them for and why I wouldn't have recorded them.

The drive to shop and relax convinces me to tear out the last check on that page, leave it with the receptionist, and get on with my afternoon. Surely, a margarita will help me remember. As I chasse' out the door, that new, nervous looking woman looks me straight in the eye and says hello. I thoughtlessly return her greeting with a smile, not even noting her lack of nervousness and lack of a new look.

I meet my friend and we sink into our self-care routine with laughter and drinks. As the umbrella booze arrives, I receive a call from my bookkeeper.

"There are no funds in your account," she blurts.

"What?! How can that be? I have thousands in there," I frantically reply.

"According to your books you should," she agrees.

I stammer back, "Let me call the bank."

I abruptly hang up and dial the bank. Sure enough, insufficient funds. I am cleaned out. Every last dime is gone.

"I am on my way," I shout into the receiver.

I down my drink, promise to explain on the way, and drag my girlfriend out the door. By the time I reach the bank, it is almost closing time. They let me in and we sit down. The teller tells me two checks went through within thirty minutes of each other at two different banks around 12:30 and 1:00 pm today.

I instantly connected the missing checks from earlier. "This was theft," I shout. "I didn't write those checks."

While the bankers initiate the fraud filing process, I start to cry as I think about payroll on Monday and the bills I have to pay. I have no money. They say there was nothing that they can do until they investigate more. They advise me to file a report with the police so I drive straight there after the bank. A detective is to call me on Monday. For now, I wait.

I wipe away tears as I drive home dumbfounded and worried. Who would do this? And how am I am going to pay my employees? I don't know if my sense of failed responsibility or betrayal is stronger at that moment, but they are both big.

Monday morning, the bank calls with more bad news. My debit card is being declined. I look in my wallet and see that it is missing. I thought, *DEAR GOD, hit me again*!

They put a hold on it and have me come back to the bank to file a report. As I am sitting in the bank, the detective calls and asks to meet. We make plans to meet at the salon in an hour. Meanwhile, the bank is getting the camera footage on the drive through. After a weekend of waiting, I feel that I am getting somewhere.

I meet a very handsome and polite detective and relay the whole story. He asks where I keep my wallet and my check book. Of course, he thinks it was one of my employees. I don't want to believe that any of them would steal from me. I remember all my employees were at the salon on Friday and the checks went through around 12:30 pm. I was hopeful it couldn't be anyone so close.

He said he will track down the card and see where it was used and he will look at the surveillance cameras and get back with me. Meanwhile, I am in debt up to my eye balls!

Within a week the bank and the detective call. They were working together to figure this out. Whoever took it had spent $3,200 from my checking account and another $1,500 on my charge card.

The detective met me at the bank and asked if I recognize the person in the surveillance tape. They blow it up and I look closely, thinking she looks familiar and then I remember… The random face from that Friday.

"She looked nervous," I offer.

"I have a hunch that it's an inside job. Could she be a friend of one of your employees?" His dark eyes flicker with the thrill of the hunt. It is a glorious diversion for that very brief moment to see this beautiful man so intent on rescuing me from this mess. "I'll need to come in and interview all the employees," he insists as I swooned.

When he enters the salon that next Tuesday morning with the sun flickering through the double doors behind him, providing a glowing aura that stops my heart, I think, I deserve this. If I have to be robbed and have my entire life turned upside down, this very attractive young detective is the least the universe can provide me as a consolation prize.

One by one, the hairdressers and nail techs come in and notice the good-looking fixture in the back of the salon posed in a military stance. "Employee meeting," I announce as I gather all of them in the back room, introducing Mike, the detective. He explains the situation in a curt and matter of fact way that strikes me as so powerful. My employees shift from intrigue at this delectably handsome man to offence at the realization that he is here to investigate each of them.

He is good at his job. It turns out he was right about it being an inside job, although how much my employee actually knew will be a mystery forever. Mike traced the clues and concluded the thief was a friend of a friend. I am conflicted with the satisfaction of getting closer to the thief and the betrayal of my friend. She swears to this day that she didn't know. And maybe she didn't.

Time passes really slowly after that. Mike calls every week to keep me updated and sometimes to inform me there was nothing new to update me on. Then, I start to cut his hair. The money hasn't been returned and the caper hasn't been solved, but I have a lovely new friend to keep me company through it all.

A few more months pass before he bursts into the salon and announces, "I have good news." His steamy smile punctuates the grand declaration, "We arrested her today!"

I stop mid snip and freeze. When I gather my faculties, I dash over to him and wrap my arms around his strong shoulders as tears fill my eyes. "Now what?" I ask inches from his face, all the emotions pulsating.

Eventually, he explains that the crime ring is made up of a group of four - two women and two men. They are real professionals. They hit at least twelve businesses in the past few months. My mouth drops. They are in jail and a trial date is set. But, "dear," he informs me, "you will have to testify."

Oh, hell yes, I will, I think, until he informs me that the others refused to out of fear of repercussion. My heart stops, "Really? Should I be worried?"

He grabs my hand and assures me I will be safe. "Please testify. If no one does, they might go free. They might get away with it. We have to put them away."

Six months pass and it is the day of the trial. I am the only one that showed up to give my testimony. I wear all black and high heels. I need to feel strong and look broken. Black always does that for me. By the time I arrive in the courtroom, I am so scared my stomach is churning. Mike meets me at the door and offers a calming hug. "You're making a difference. Be proud of yourself." I almost throw up on his shoes.

Inside the court room, I eye my assailant. She is shackled and in orange with the rest of her accomplices. She stares intently at the floor. I keep my gaze on her for the entirety of the court proceedings. I think or hope that she will look at me and I will be able to understand why she did this and simultaneously convey to her how much she took from me. I want her to be a person and I want empathy to cross between us in some silent way. But as the lawyers lay out the charges, over a million dollars of other people's work, I start to get angry. I worked and dreamed and sacrificed for this business and they are getting rich off my achievements. My head starts to spin. I was red with anger when I hear my name called. I walk over to the judge and swear myself in. At the podium, I settle myself just enough to summon my voice. It cracks and shakes, then the tears begin. With a deep breath, I steady my nerves and refocus my intention. *Don't cry. Get mad.* So, with the force of a sledge hammer, I pound out my story.

I speak with passion of the deep wounds she inflicted. I tell the judge I am a single mom with three kids and that she just didn't just steal from my business and my employees, she stole from my kids, my family. I confess the fear of losing it all. I confess the shame of having to borrow money from my parents to pay my employees, feed my kids, and to put gas in my car because she took every dime I had. She must not realize when she stole from one fancy business, she was stealing from all of us – stealing money and dreams and safety and pride. Her impact was huge and I will never forgive or forget this. I hammer in that as a single woman owning a business, it was hard enough. But shame on her, stealing from another women that is only trying to make a living in this world and to raise my kids and have a roof over their heads. And she tried to take that from me and my family.

I end with, "I stand here today for all 12 of us that they stole from. To make a difference and to make them accountable of the wrong doing. It has taken me months to get my business back running and my kids are terrified. I hope when I leave this court room today that justice is served." With this she finally meets my eyes. There is nothing passed between us, no understanding or forgiveness. I have found my revival in my own anger and strength and resilience. I don't need her remorse. I am filled with my own resolve.

They were given seven years. I was given my money and my spirit back.

The Favorites

"Life is too short to have boring hair."

-Unknown

"I am booked solid next week, dear," I fib through a saccharine sweet smile.

What's one little white lie compared to my mental health, right? Some clients are hard - hard to please, hard to read, hard to stand.

But, on the flip side of that, some clients make my day come alive. I live for their smiles and stories. I go out of my way to make special time for those clients. I bump people out, stay late, or even *gasp* come in early for them. I (mostly) willingly come in on Mondays, my only day off, if they need me because I love them like family.

My cache of beauties consisted of quite a lot of "snowbirds" in Phoenix. They flocked in around October as the weather cooled to a point of light cardigan bliss and held steady through the winter months. They hailed from up North or back East and reveled in the temperate climate. My life got very busy at that time of the year, with 10–12-hour days to get them all in.

I have my favorites; the ones I enjoy their company as much as their business. These rare birds are such a gift to spend an afternoon with, that I don't even squeeze anyone in while their color sits. I soak up every minute I can spend in their presence. I hug and kiss them when they arrive and revel in their stories, attitudes, and essences. They are all types – young, old, rich, poor. It is much more about the way they do life than their specific details of existence. Energetic connections transcend age, race, class, and gender.

The variety of souls that graced my chair was bountiful. There was Cheryl and Carol, the lesbian couple that took me shopping and taught me so much about politics, health, exercise, food, and love. We laughed and even cried together as kindred spirits do.

There was Bennie, from the Bronx. Since I am Italian, we hit it off right away. He was a flirt. He loved to sing and eat! He would come in without an appointment and I would "fit" him in every time. We had many deep conversations of me finding my "center". I felt safe enough to talk to him about my driving force and personal values. He couldn't wrap his head around what "my center" meant, but he always checked in with my search for it. I loved him like an uncle. He wasn't happy in his marriage and he confided in me about an affair he was having. I was forced to rethink the strict definitions I had come to understand of right and wrong and simply be happy for him because he was happy. His laugh was infectious. It was right from his belly and his heart was as big as his smile. He was the best hugger. We told each other things that I would never tell anyone else. He trusted me as much as I trusted him.

Then there was Julia. Italian and Greek women get along like peanut butter and jelly. We both like to talk loudly and use our hands to accentuate points. There was a sisterly connection there, like when you can fall back into a memory and every detail is understood like they were part of it. We just got each other. We were ten years apart in age but it didn't matter. She was the best dressed client I had. She drove fancy cars and was always going somewhere exciting. She loved getting pampered. She also was a creature of (hair) habit. One year, I convinced her to grow out her "Dumb and Dumber" bangs. It was a hard-fought battle of wills and commitment. She gives me shit every time she comes in for a color and begs me to cut them. I said no and surprisingly, she stuck it out. I personally love being right, and eventually, she gave me all the credit.

She would settle into my chair and say, "Why the hell did you let me look like 'Dumb and Dumber' for so long?"

I would shrug and say, "The client always knows best." Then I would wink and smack her. Laughter and goofy haircuts aside, it was about trust. She was committed to a choice (a mistake I would say) and it was through smiles and prodding and patience that we grew to trust each other. She trusted me with her style, her presentation to the world, and

I know I earned that by being consistent and steadfast. She was another one that told me things no one ever knew. Story after story. Year after year.

One of my very favorite clients, Mildred, was 73 years old. She came in every week on Thursday at 9:00 am. I primped her for about ten years. She was in shape, always dressed very hip, loved the sun so she was dramatically tan, a widow, avid bridge player, and loved her scotch on the rocks every day at 5:00 pm. She was always giving me advice in a peculiarly loving way. Her classical politeness kept her silent for nearly a year of visits. After we really got to know each other, the gates were flung open, and the most entrancing stories and perspectives would seep out of her timid frame. She maintained a youthful and energetic nature by traveling and keeping up with her grandkids. I admired her gentleness and her sweet laugh. She never missed an opportunity to bring food and recipes. Our hugs got longer as time went on and the audible hellos and goodbyes were dropped. She listened to all my stories with such grace. She listened to laugh or guide, never to judge. I always wondered why certain people come into our lives and I always feel she was an angel. She was so wise, so gentle, and so sincere. Her passing left me crushed and eternally grateful in a swirling mix of big emotions.

Cindy was 79 years old when I started doing her up-do every week. Up-dos are not my thing. I grit my teeth through my own grandmother's up-do once a year and it takes a bottle of wine and a shopping trip to recover. When this particular client came my way, let's just say it wasn't peanut butter and jelly, as much as hot sauce and macaroni cheese. She was a pistol. She shot from the hip with every word. There was no filter... Ever. I never did her hair right and she would complain before she left and complain when she showed up the following week. It was hard and humiliating. But, somehow, I loved her brand of bitter crazy. She was aggressive but velvety. She had a roughness that was tempered with flair. It was dysfunction from the first appointment. Most of the time I kept trying to pawn her off on someone else but everyone avoided her like a hot curling iron in the lap.

So, I kept her. I tried to find the good in her. She was miserable. She was angry. She was negative. She was old. I mustered compassion for her and never took it personally. After about 6 months, I really was immune to all her venom. I just let her talk and kept doing her hair the way I wanted and she kept coming back. I guess that was a sign she liked me. She didn't know how to be nice. It wasn't in her nature. When I came to grips with that, I loved her. She decided to start dating at 80 years old. I thought, you go girl, and boy did she. Week after week, I heard stories of these old folks getting it on.

I kept prying, "But, how?"

She said, "Honey, it's all in the woman."

I replied, "What does that mean?"

She would wink and then wave her hand over her body like Vanna White and say, "How could they resist this?!"

I would laugh until I couldn't stand up. Once I adjusted my attitude and figured out a way around her abrasive exterior, she became one of my favorites each week.

Everything happens for a reason but in my case, *everyone* happened for a reason. That reason - I need them as much as they need me.

The Story Hour

"Getting your hair done is like having a mini-vacation."

-Unknown

Bad days, good days, Thursdays…any day is a good day for a martini.

It was a typical work week with the busyness of business and my mother calling to barge in because one of her bingo friends died and she needs to be ready for the funeral.

She never misses a funeral or bingo on Wednesdays at the church's club house.

My phone buzzes in my pocket.

"Honey, you need to squeeze me in. I have a funeral on Thursday," She shouts into my ear.

I pause for a moment, "Didn't you just go to one last week?"

She replies, "can you squeeze me in or not?"

"I can squeeze you in tomorrow morning while a color is sitting," I offer.

"Oh, you know that won't work. I have Bingo at 11:00," She scolds, then pushes, "look again, any time after 2:30 will do."

I say, "I have to pick up Grace at 3:30 and take her to the dentist by 4:00."

She calmly replied, "I knew you had time. I will tell your father to take her to the dentist and then you can do my hair."

Wednesday rolls around and she bounds in 30 minutes early, walks over to my station and asks assumingly, "You ready for me?"

"No."

I try to look busy, but she caught me in a rare moment of being ahead of schedule and I feel my coveted break slipping through my fingers. She looks around and sees no one in the waiting area, no one under the dryer. Her eyes flash as she sits down and motions for me to get on with it.

"You won't believe what your father did yesterday!" I make the beginning sounds of a guess, but she cuts me off as she fumbles through her purse. "Yesterday morning, I thought I would iron all our clothes in the bedroom so I can watch my soap opera while your father is watching his show." I open my mouth to interject a well-placed snarky comment, when she interrupts, "Are you going to shampoo me or what?"

I wave her to the back of the room. She lies back in the shampoo bowl and continues her story like a geyser of gossip. She raises her voice to hear herself over the sprayer and proceeds to obliviously include the entire salon in her audience. I lock eyes with the bewildered onlookers and shrug.

"I am minding my business, ironing our clothes and your father walks in the bedroom, smiles, and winks."

I interject, "At least he was in a good mood!" but, she ignores my comment and keeps on talking. I continue to shampoo her hair.

"Now, I just keep ironing and ignore him, and he walks over to me and gets really close."

I butt in and ask, "how close?"

"Close! He is standing right next to me," she exclaims, head tilted back, volume on high.

"Was he trying to get your attention or something?" I wonder.

She holds her hand up. "Get me out of this shampoo bowl."

I shut off the water, wrap her head with a towel, and then she whispers, "I don't want everyone to hear me." Our audience quickly diverts their eyes.

She sits back into my chair, I spray some mouse on her hair, comb it, and she begins again. I flip the blow dryer on like a curtain of privacy and I lean in so she doesn't have to shout. She shouts.

"I am ironing away, and I look over at him. He is right in front me, he smiles, and I smell alcohol. I gasped, 'Are you drinking this morning?' He smiled and before I could think he smacks my ass!"

"What? Mom, he slaps your ass like a friendly slap or pissed off slap?" I inquire, trying to feel this out.

She snaps, "Who the hell cares, he slapped my ass! Quit interrupting me."

"I am trying to have a conversation with you. I can't ask questions?" I ask, knowing the answer already.

"Shut up and let me talk." She goes on as I roll my eyes and stand up straight. She's not whispering anymore, so no need to make pretenses.

She proceeds, "After he slaps my ass, I said 'what the hell are you doing?' He didn't say a word. He just did it again!"

Now, I stop the blow dryer, stand in front of her, make an inquisitive expression, and wait.

"He wanted to have whoopee!" She yells into the void of hairdryer noise.

"Does that mean sex?" I ask, trying to translate her old-timey lingo (or maybe take a cheap shot at her age).

She kept her head down. "Yes," she replies shamefully. "We haven't had sex in ten years. Where is this coming from?"

"Well, I don't find that romantic." I cringe as I picture the scene.

"Romantic?!" she blurted, "I said 'What the hell do you want? I am ironing here!' Then your father said, 'Let's do it' and shook his hips at me like a geriatric gigolo." She crossed her arms over her chest and turned her head away.

I stood for a moment, mouth agape, unable to respond in a helpful way. Then, I decide to respond in the most unhelpful way. "Listen, you are grossing me out. I don't want to know about you guys having sex at your age!"

Oh, dear God, wrong thing to say, I thought as I saw her eyes flash in the mirror. She sat very still - fuming, then whips her chair around to face me and growls between gritted teeth, "What do you mean 'at your age?'"

I gulp and boldly reply, "You're old," with a shrug that, turns out, did not lessen the blow.

The silence. The smoldering glare. "I. Am. Not. Old." she retorted as she raised one eyebrow in a menacing expression of roiling rage.

"Ok, ok, I take that back, but don't you think it might be a bit dried up?" I ask with a disbelieving look. Meanwhile, a few coworkers heard what I said and stopped their blow dryers to see how this conversation is going to play out. We are all looking to at her, my mother, the story teller of our family's dirty business.

She wrung her hands shifted her seat, noticing the quiet in the salon. Everyone busied themselves, avoiding eye contact, but proved to be quite bad at acting. I flick my head in a covert attempt to rid my mother of their attention because I wasn't going to get the rest of this story like this.

So, I said, "Is there more to this story?"

She pulls her lips into a pout, then drops her head in her chest, sighs deeply, and goes on. "I slam the iron down." she says through gritted teeth, "walk into the living room and I see the vodka on the counter." She motions as if there were vodka in front of us, and I can't help but wish there was. "Your dad is right behind me like a chipper puppy. I said 'are you crazy drinking at 11:00 in the morning with all your medication? You could have a stroke!' He winks and beacons, 'Come on, let's do it…. Come on…. Come on. What's the big deal?' I look at him said 'Come on? Do you think that's going to work?'"

"So, did you?" I need to know exactly where this story is going. I'm formulating a visual of my parents doing it and starting to feel a bit queasy.

She snaps, "HELL NO! I had ironing to do and lunch plans with my friends."

I have never felt more relieved.

"But wait, there is more," she says, halting my contentment.

143

She relays with great dismay how the scene played out. "I go into the kitchen and see the vodka on the counter and turn to yell at him, but he is right behind me. It scared the shit out of me. I jumped and pulled my back out a bit."

I briefly think of an alternate way she could have strained her back and am so thankful it was just fear. I shake my head as I begin curling her hair. She goes on.

"He leans into me, breathing heavily on my neck, puts his hands on my hip bones and pushes me against the counter," she says incredulously.

"Let me stop you right there." I say stepping back a few feet.

She says, "Really Mia, don't be so prude."

I put the curling iron down and, like the sophisticated professional I am, I plug my ears, close my eyes and frantically shake my head back and forth, humming, then yelling into the void, "Please, don't say anything about his private parts."

"I don't have all day here," she chides me to get back to her hair.

"Really? You're going to say that to me?" I say with my hand on my cocked hip. "I think I should be saying that to you."

She goes on, "I told him to get off me. I had things to do and he says 'let's do those things.' Ewww," she says.

144

Ewww, indeed.

"Then he slapped my ass."

"What?!?"

"So, I slapped his back." She paused for unnecessary effect, "Unfortunately, he liked it."

"Mom. Stop. Talking." I plead.

"Did you at least remind him to get Grace today?" I say, hoping to change the subject.

"Yes. He didn't remember me telling him yesterday that he needs to do that for you."

I remind her, "well, it was for you - so you could get your hair done."

"Oh noooo, I didn't tell him that," she corrects like I had suggested something ludicrous. "He wouldn't have done it. I knew he would do it if I told him you had to work."

"But I'm working on you," I say. "He is going to notice you got your hair done."

"Oh honey, no he won't," she lets a bitter laugh and I feel a bit sorry for her (opposed to myself) for the first time during that story. "He doesn't look at me that way. He never notices the big things like a color or perm, so why would he notice my hair is pretty? It's quite convenient, really."

"Dear God, you both are pieces of work," I whisper under my breath.

My phone rings and we both know instantly who it is. "Hey Dad, thanks for getting Grace."

"Are you with mom?" He asks.

She hits me in the arm, furiously shaking her head. "Don't tell him I am here," she hisses.

"No?" My lie is so pitiful, I can't help but giggle at myself. "Hey Dad, how are you feeling today? Is everything good?" My mom slaps me again on the arm.

"Why, yes I am great now. Funny you should ask, though, I was moving slow this morning and had a bit of headache. But, it's nothing a few Tylenol can't take care of."

"I can think of a few other things that will take care of a headache" I say, winking at my mom.

She slaps my ass.

"Oh, I have a headache too," I say to both of them.

"I will leave you some Tylenol on your counter, then," he kindly offers.

"And, I'll wash it down with some Vodka," I say as I hang up the phone.

Survival

"Her messy hair a visible attribute of her stubborn spirit.

As she shakes it free, she smiles knowing wild is her

favorite color."

-Unknown

Survival is the name of the river I floated for the eleven years I owned the salon.

An impending divorce and the strife that accompanies that fed into an actual divorce and the shitstorm that ushers that back up the aisle. But, for better or worse, the salon was solely mine three years in. A real business woman should have a degree, I thought, so I went back to school to see if respect and power could be found in those books. I was formulating a backup plan with a sober understanding that I wouldn't cut hair forever. That plan fluctuated from an interior design degree (but the math was not my specialty), to art history (it was way too deep for me) and then, finally, I found my calling to become a counselor. Going to school, raising three kids, owning a business, juggling men, even the things I did solely for me – gym at 4am, yoga on the weekends-were becoming exhausting. The grind was grinding me.

When I thought I had sunk below the surface and couldn't find the will to pull myself up, yet again, the father of one of my girlfriends offered to help me. He offered fatherly wisdom and advice and kindly took on my books. I was so grateful for the help.

You're not making any money, he advised. You have to live off your payments from behind the chair. You need to build the business up. Everything goes back into the business. I remember thinking, I own a house, have a car payment, and kids are expensive. I can't live off that. He took me by the shoulders, looked deep into my scared eyes and said it's the only thing you can do to move forward. So, I did. We ate a lot of macaroni and cheese. Pizza night was only if I had a good week. We sacrificed the comforts we had come to know. We sacrificed our present for our future.

I was struggling. My hours were long, my kids needed clothes. I needed a break, a lucky break.

I remember the sticky, sweaty, endless drudgery of the summer when he came to me with the business proposition. "An investment," he said with wide excited eyes, "that I could get you in on." You see, his friend Walt handled all the family's money. I was lucky to be invited into their club. Walt would take my investment and triple it, quadruple it. This was my shot, I thought. I've known this man since I was fourteen. He drove me around town, I had sleepovers with his kid. He was giving me the opportunity I had begged and prayed for. So, I gave him my savings. Ten thousand dollars. This is going to lift me out of survival mode. With this, I am going to be able to breathe again. I'm going to thrive. Did I lose sleep giving my life savings over to ole' one-name "Walt"? Nope.

Christmas was approaching and with it the stress of holiday cheer, that mom is financially and emotionally responsible for, the hustle and bustle of holiday parties that clients must look their best for, the sick and traveling employees, and all the other merriment that comes with the most wonderful time of year. Not a moment too soon, in walks my fatherly adviser with a fat check in his hands. Our Christmas was made! We were going to celebrate like old times. Presents, decorations, drinks, and no mac and cheese to be seen. "This was smart, kid," he said. "You will make a lot of money if you stick with me." He hugged and kissed me, beaming with pride and joy. We both knew how much this money meant to me.

My book keeper called a week after Christmas. "My numbers and their numbers are off."

"How off?" I asked.

"It's not small," she said. "We're missing thousands of dollars."

I desperately called my friend and told him what was happening. "There is no way it is off. She is wrong," he insisted.

Next, I heard I owe the IRS over $8,000.00! How can this be happening? I could lose everything. I've been pinching pennies for months and now I have even less than I started with.

Everyone was pointing the finger at someone else. My accountant accused me of hiding money. I accused my friend's dad of something nefarious.

After I addressed the issue with my friend's Dad, he got mad. He was irate. He said all of the curse words. I said them all back. I fired him from doing my books.

I had to schedule monthly payments to the IRS for the next year. I used some of the Christmas money I got back from my "investment" to help pay. I had never felt stress like this before. I lost sleep and weight and friends. I was crumbling under the weight of it all.

But, somehow, I kept putting one foot in front of the other. A couple months after I fired this guy, my salon was in full swing and I finally felt like I was back on track. One chipper morning the salon phone rang before it was open. It was my friend's Dad.

"I have some news," he somberly announced.

"What could it possibly be?" I wondered aloud with all the disdain I could muster.

"You know your investment I made for you? Well, you know I mentioned the name "Wayne" to you?" He paused for a long time, then continued, his voice breaking, "He hung himself last night."

I gasped.

Then it all came rushing out so fast, "He spent all our money! It is all gone. Every cent." He was crying and banging his fist on something on the other end of the line.

I remember standing at the front desk, holding my breath, a rush of heat came over me, my vision started to dim. I thought I would throw up. I drew in a deep shaky breath with my eyes closed down tight. I fought for a last moment of peace before I allowed the full weight of the news to absorb me. As I let it out, the feelings of dread, of betrayal, of despair welled up inside me.

"Did you hear me?" I heard an echo of the man's voice through the phone asking.

I replied with a faint, "yes."

And though I didn't need to hear it again, he repeated "your money is gone. All our money."

"I trusted you," I managed. Then I slowly hung up the phone.

The shameful tears overtook me standing there at the front desk. What a fool I was. I sobbed myself into a heap on the salon floor.

It was many years later when I heard about another guy that stole everyone's money in New York. I had a visceral reaction to the news that day. I remembered the shame and guilt I felt for allowing myself to be swindled. I remembered the hatred I felt for that thief. Wayne was my Bernie Madoff.

Meditation or Medicine

Hair- dress –er /noun/ "a magician who creates a hair

style you can never duplicate."

-Fun Definitions.com

Classically, "yoga" is translated to mean "union" or "yoking" in English. To me it means "relationship." Yoga taught me to learn about myself. It taught me to listen to the chatter within my mind and explore the reasons why I allow it to change my day when it is not serving me. Yoga taught me to accept myself and to have an awareness of the way in which I react to the events of my day. Most of all, it taught me to remember that everything is impermanent and with that realization, I stopped suffering.

Meditation is the hardest form of yoga. The first few years... I sucked at it. I kept failing and telling myself it is impossible. My teacher insisted I could do it... Begin again and again and again. "One day you will sit and in the moment it will happen. You feel lifted or awakened," she would say. "Then it will be like a drug. You will want to do it more and more."

I was drawn to yoga for the physical attributes. I complained about my back and my feet hurting constantly from standing in heels all day. Someone recommended it and I thought, *what the hell?*

During my first class, I thought I was going to DIE! But, I went back. I started with one day per week to see if it made me feel better. I noticed that I did *feel* different on that day of the week – lighter, freer. So, I bumped it up to two days per week, then three. I got hooked.

Having three kids, a boyfriend that traveled all the time, my own salon, and myself to handle meant that I needed an escape. Not a week-long vacation to get a grip, but a real place of solitude and peace. I needed a place that provided a head space. I needed to lay down, be still, and have someone else tell me what to do. And oh, that was hard.

Hairdressers hold space for everyone. It is exhausting. I listen to people's personal stories and issues like they are confessions. Scandal, secrets, heartbreak, loss – I bared it all for ten hours per day. Some people work with their hands, some with their heads, I work with my heart. Yoga solidified the idea for me that people are literally draining me, energetically. I felt so heavy after a day at the salon because of the drama (not necessarily the standing in heels).

I learned that movement heals the body, but stillness heals the mind. That was powerful for me. I wanted more. Yoga became my obsession, my drug - my release and escape, but also my sanctuary and healer.

I could get on my mat and let everything go. My body would scream for the first few minutes of physical practice, but then it was like flowing in the wind for the rest of the class.

Meditation occurred at the end of class. We would sit for fifteen minutes and the instructor would guide us most of the time. Sometimes she would be silent. We would all be silent. This was the most challenging yoga I did.

Years later, I realized why it was so hard to sit still. Stillness steals from us the ability to avoid ourselves, to avoid the negative stuff life brings us – trauma, abuse, neglect. We keep moving to avoid the real stuff of ourselves. When we sit in stillness, we have to hear the music, face the shit, deal with it. My shit would bubble up more than I want to admit.

I used shopping, men, food, and alcohol as avenues to avoid the mess. I refused to face any of it. Soon, the music was so loud, I had to listen.

Yoga saved my life. It saved me from me.

Just when I think I have it all figured out, though, when I feel healed from my past and stable in myself, it all bubbles up again. And again, I begin…

Peace

"Blondes are noticed but redheads are remembered."

-Unknown

I am a seeker of peace. I longed for equanimity through it all. I was clawing and hustling my way through. Each day failed to register as a success, just a near miss. Sure, I laughed and loved, but I yearned for the restful realization that I was alright.

I was doing it wrong, they said. Everyone seemed to be telling me how to live, who to date, what to wear, how to raise my kids. I was tracing the perimeter of a good life, but just never found myself swaddled safely in the middle of it. Not for lack of trying.

I always thought when I get a man and settle down again, I'll find peace.

I thought when the salon makes more money, I'll have peace.

I thought when the kids are a little older, I'll know peace.

I thought yoga would awaken peace within me.

"Peace" was my mantra; the word that I repeated, the concept I obsessed over. I would sit on my front porch with a glass of wine gripped in my hand as a life line to an unraveling, an emotional state of sanctity and safety, all the while rocking myself in an attempt to soothe the fear and tears away. I sent up the same prayer every time: let me feel peace.

Sometimes it's the smallest of decisions that changes your life course. It's not the one you obsess over for hours, it's the one you put absolutely no thought into, stumble in only prepared with who you are at the most basic level. It was a new yoga studio for me. I went alone, not by design, but because no friends were available. It was surprisingly small. The entire studio was a closet compared to my standards. The instructor emerged from a back room, a full foot shorter than me. In broken English, she said, "let us begin." There was no one else in the place. It would have only been slightly more awkward if I had scooped up my things and dashed out. As it was, I stayed.

She offered no music, no props, no towel or any of the accessories that turned out to be quite comforting to me. She instructed me to stand at the front of my mat in Tadasana - Mountain pose. I obeyed. She broke into a chant which sounded both exotic and exhilarating. I tried to push the fear and discomfort down by replacing it with a willingness to be open to new experiences. I tried. But, then, she simply instructed me to "begin." Begin what? I just stared at her in silent confusion, and she stared at me in silent disgust (I assumed). She poked, pushed, and said "no" for the next hour, pose after pose.

Why the hell am I here? I wonder. I can't even walk out because it is only me and her. I am getting angrier by the minute. In yoga, I know I am supposed to concentrate on my breath, but I fixate on the clock. I know I am supposed to clear my mind, but I flood it with - inhale: "I am," exhale: "never coming back."

It was the longest hour of my life. I couldn't get out of there fast enough. When it was over, I grabbed my mat, wadded it under my arm, sheepishly thanked her for a lovely class and bolted for the door, solidifying in my mind how not-lovely the class was.

I put my head down and rushed to my car. My head is spinning reliving the torturous hour I just endured. "No" this and "No" that. I grab my door handle and there she is like a ghost. I didn't even hear her behind me. I jumped back at her sudden appearance and just stared, frozen in the parking lot.

She leans in really close and says with quiet conviction, "why did you come here today?"

I didn't have a coherent thought past, what the fuck, so I didn't say anything for quite a while. She held the line and waited for me to get it together. Finally, I replied, "I am looking for peace."

She pursed her lips then said, "you don't find peace there," pointing at the studio. She readied her well exercised poking finger and once again prodded into me, this time shaping my form deeply. "You find peace here," she said with her finger in my chest, quite profoundly touching my heart.

My eyes immediately welled up with tears. She saw her message had landed so she turned and walked away. I cried all the way home. What did she mean? I find peace here? I gripped my chest as if she had punctured my heart.

For so long, I pursued my peace through attention - I looked for it in men, I chased it in the form of success. I thought my girlfriends, my business, my kids, my home, my money was where it hid. I just needed more, more of all those external things. Then I'd be happy.

I was so struck by the message that woman conveyed that I started desperately searching for it in yoga. I acquired book after book. I poured over YouTube videos. I perfected poses. I truly didn't get it. I was such a mess internally and I didn't know how to get out of the darkness. I didn't know how to put down this burden of fear, shame, guilt, and sadness.

I was searching for it in everything around me, but there it was in the one place I hadn't stopped to look at. It came when I sat and listened to my inner child. It came when I held the space long enough to let her heal. The asana, the sweat, the breath was all a vehicle to get to my center and to prepare me for what I would experience there.

When I was anxious or frustrated, I knew yoga was my path to calm, centered equanimity. When I was feeling insecure, heavy, or fearful, I practiced yoga and left feeling blissful. It was beautiful. I learned later in life that I am in control of my peace. I floundered when I searched for it in men and money. But, now I know where it stays. I simply have to choose to journey inward and commit to the practice. It is not always easy, but I know now that peace is within me and I carry its potential always. I was forty-two years old when I discovered peace in my heart and ever since I have worked to tame my inner shadow. Most of the time I feel that shadow is gone and all that remains is light, love, and peace. It is daily work.

The shift occurred first inside, then manifested itself in huge life changes that perpetuated the healing. I sold the salon. I moved to Texas. I broke the energy patterns, the biology patterns. I was finally free to be me. Forty-two was a magical number. I became a yoga teacher. Yoga saved me from me. It woke me up like nothing else in my life ever did.

The salon was a labor of love - hard labor and intense love. It was a constant struggle to keep it afloat, maintain employees, keep it clean, but it did bring me such joy, laughter, great friends and a satisfying career. Along the way, I picked up some virtues I'm eternally grateful for. Grit, gumption, and persistence don't come for free. My salon led me to yoga. Without it, I would never have found me in this whole story. Yoga is the duality of light and darkness and the balance of the two. We are not whole without both of those sides.

Love and Peace is my signature. Gratitude is in my heart and light is all I see.

Namaste